Shady Agents™

How to Sell Your Home Using Agents, Appraisers, Home Inspectors and Other Rats

Licensed Real Estate Broker

SLICK SHYSTER

Shady Agents™

How to Sell Your Home Using Agents, Appraisers, Home Inspectors and Other Rats

Dedicated to

Crime Victim Advocate Debbie McGowan

Table of Contents

AGENT-SELECTION PHASE CHAPTERS:

Spouses That Sell Houses

Corporate Loafers

Old Timers

The Burned-Out Broker

Loners

Promoters

Newbies

The Busybody Soccer Mom

Incompetent Drama Queens

Greedy Agents

LISTING PHASE CHAPTERS:

NEGOTIATING PHASE CHAPTERS:

UNDER-CONTRACT PHASE CHAPTERS:

Introduction

How-to real estate books written by top-selling agents explain the home-selling process but provide little insight about the role of the agent. As you can tell by its title, this book underscores the impact agents have upon the transaction. It is a behind-the-scenes look at the home-selling process and warns what can go wrong and what to expect from licensed real estate agents.

The chapters of this book are in sequential order reflecting the phases of the transaction:

- ✓ Prelisting phase (chapters 1-6).

- ✓ Agent-selection phase (chapters 7-9).

- ✓ Listing phase (chapters 10-20).

- ✓ Selling phase (chapters 21-27).

- ✓ Negotiating phase (chapters 28-32).

- ✓ Under-contract phase (chapters 33-36).

- ✓ Closing phase (chapters 37-39).

- ✓ Complaint phase (chapters 40-42).

This book does not delve into felonious crimes like loan or title fraud. It explains the chicanery and/or incompetence of the repeat offenders who escape justice and remain selling for years. The book makes good study for agents pursuing a noble and rewarding career helping people buy and sell houses and broker-owners building an organization with a positive moral purpose.

All the advice and examples provided are drawn from my thirty-five years of selling real estate and supervising agents. Nothing has been made up. Where possible I support my claims with research performed by outside sources and do my best to separate what really sells a home from the baloney promulgated by Shady Agents who often say,

"Just get the deal done; no one gets paid for being honest."

(PRELISTING PHASE)

1
CHAPTER

What Could Go Wrong

You may begin selling your home as a FSBO (for sale by owner). But as a FSBO your home will not be in the local multiple listing service (MLS) database owned and operated by local brokers. Without MLS you will probably promote your home with newspaper ads, Craigslist and some sort of FSBO website. You may soon find ads only attract quirky buyers looking for bargains. Eventually you will call an agent, even though the thought of paying a 5 percent or 6 percent commission makes you wince.

When the prospective agent completes a tour of your home, he or she will begin what is known as the "listing presentation". At this point, much of what any agent says is premeditated with the aim of getting your signature on a listing contract.

If you ask about discounting the commission, the agent may offer to reduce the so-called "standard" 6 percent commission to 5 percent.[1] What you do not know is that it is illegal for agents

to imply the commission is "standard" or set by some governmental authority because the law dictates that all commissions are negotiable. Nevertheless, you will probably rationalize the commission will be recouped by the high price the agent says you can get for the home.

---

[1] 7 percent and 6 percent are considered top rates. A commission of 4 percent or less is considered a discounted rate.

After signing the listing contract, you assume your agent has your best interests at heart and foolishly surrender control of the entire process to the agent, making you susceptible to many nasty surprises:

✓ Before you signed the listing agreement, the agent explained how her large firm with national exposure would get you top dollar. But as the months pass with no offers, the agent changes her tune and now says your home is overpriced.

✓ A day after signing the agent's listing contract, some broker you never heard of delivers a full-price offer. You'll scratch your head and wonder what your listing agent did to earn the $28,000 commission.

✓ Your agent promised to handle all appointments. But when months pass with no showings, you call your agent only to find his voicemail is always full.

✓ Months after listing your home, you get a copy of the MLS data sheet and discover there is only one photo, the directions to your home are wrong, and it's listed in the condo section of the MLS database and not under single-family homes where it belongs.

✓ Disappointed by a low offer, you learn your listing agent is telling other agents you are "desperate to sell."

✓ You sell your home for less than asking price to a buyer delivered by your listing agent. You later hear another agent had a full-price offer for your home, but to protect her own offer, your listing agent told the other agent your home had already been sold.

✓ You need to move quickly, so you ask your agent to list your home both for sale *and* for rent. You will accept a buyer or tenant—whichever arrives first. What you don't know is that to earn the larger sales commission, your agent changed the status of your home in the rental section of MLS to "RENTED" making it appear the home is only available for sale.

✓ Your agent promised to feature your home with a photo in the local paper, but when you look, it's never there.

✓ After buyers visit your home, you ask your agent for feedback. Your agent claims the buyers complained your home is too small and overpriced. What you do not know is that the agent is lying to convince you to lower your price.

✓ You sold your home to buyers who are trying to break the contract. When you threaten to keep their deposit money, you discover none exists because your agent never told you their check was no good.

CHAPTER 1

✓ You signed a contract based on the buyers' loan prequalification letter. Your agent claimed the letter "guarantees" the buyers will get a loan. But days before the closing, you learn the bank will not issue a commitment because the buyers' credit file contains a bankruptcy. Your agent nervously laughs and says, "No one ever told me."

✓ Weeks after your home is sold, you receive a call from a second appraiser requesting to inspect your home. When you ask your agent about this second appraiser, your agent tells you not to worry, as the buyers are only changing their "loan program" to obtain a lower interest rate. In reality, the buyers were turned down by their bank and have applied to another. Not knowing the truth, you sign a contract to buy another home. When the second bank refuses to approve the buyers' loan, the contract is canceled, forcing you to forfeit the deposit on your new home.

✓ A month after your home has sold, you realize the lender never sent an appraiser. After many phone calls to your agent, the appraiser finally submits the appraisal at value lower than the contract price and the buyers refuse to close.

✓ Days before the scheduled closing, your agent says the buyers cannot get a loan. Although the agent showed you the buyers' prequalification letter, she neglected to tell you the buyer was retiring and that no lender will approve a borrower with a lack of "continued earnings." Your agent says, "Wow! I've never heard of that before."

✓ Due to a "snafu" with the buyers' loan, your closing is delayed. When you ask your agent about this, he says he will check it out and get back to you—but he never does. The episode will make you wonder why you are paying a $12,800 commission.

✓ Late one night without warning, your agent appears at your front door and says you need to sign her offer immediately. Half asleep, you ask if this can be done tomorrow but while pushing a pen in your hand all she says is "No".

✓ Hours before the closing and with your movers in your driveway, you discover a home-inspection issue concerning your roof was never formally resolved. The buyers now claim they will not close unless they receive a credit of $5,500 for a new roof.

✓ At the closing, you find your agent neglected to exclude your washer and dryer from the MLS data sheet. Now the buyers are demanding them or they will not close.

✓ At the closing, the buyers claim the window air conditioner included in the sale is missing. But you know you left it in the house when you moved out. Your agent sheepishly admits he took the air conditioner to his house for "safekeeping."

✓ After the closing you review the HUD-1 closing statement and find your agent inflated the amount she was to be paid by $3,400. When you ask for return of the overpayment, she says it's too late because the property has closed.

✓ Your vacant home has been sold, but the buyers cannot get a loan and are asking to rent the house. When you drive by the house, you discover your agent gave the buyers the key and they have moved in.

2
CHAPTER

What Makes Shady Agents Shady

Licensing laws should be easy to follow because they are in writing. On the other hand, ethical decisions are problematic because they are unwritten and based on life's lessons of right and wrong. Legally, an agent's unethical action only has consequence when it violates license law and involves: fraud, deceit, coercion, double-dealing, dishonest dealing, false promises, bad faith, failure to protect and promote, misrepresentation, comingling of funds, unworthiness, incompetence, negligence, or failure to perform a fiduciary duty.

Separation of Personal and Business Ethics

Personal ethics are basic concepts of right and wrong learned from parents, mentors and life experience. Business ethics naturally build on personal ethics. However, Shady Agents see the two as mutually exclusive. They believe laws and regulations are the only guidelines of proper business practice wherein anything goes as long as laws are not broken, i.e., nothing personal, it's just business. For example, an agent discouraging another agent's offer for your home to protect his/her own offer.

A Shady Agent's abandonment of basic, personal ethics during a transaction makes an unethical act especially unforgettable for the consumer and reinforces the negative image of all real estate agents and brokers.

Unfulfilled Promises Lead to Mistrust

Shady Agents consider the common promise of selling your home quickly and at a premium price a harmless white lie. The promise usually includes a written market analysis, qualifying buyers, providing quality photos, advertising and following up on showings. Agents usually fail to deliver on these promises until the seller complains.

Agents can be held accountable for their promises if they are put in writing and made part of the listing contract. See Chapter 13, "The Tricks and Traps of the Listing Contract".

Troubled Personal Lives

People consumed with personal problems have a hard time helping others. This is why Shady Agents will not anticipate or resolve problems without first asking, "What's in it for me?" Agents with troubled personalities are described in Chapter 9, "Shady Agent Personalities and Proclivities".

Faux Professionals

Many agents boast of their membership in the trade group known as the National Association of Realtors (NAR) because it gives them the right to call themselves professionals. But in reality they pay the yearly membership fee for the sole purpose of gaining access to the ancillary multiple listing service data base of homes (MLS). Agents who fail to see themselves providing a valued service to their clients cannot contribute to the process because the transaction is only a means to make money.

Loss of Empathy Due to Stress

The overwhelming majority of agents receive commissions sporadically. Secondly, no agent receives compensation for time spent on transactions that fail to close. This income uncertainty causes stress and depletes an agent's capacity to empathize with a client's needs leading the agent to engage in unethical acts for his/her own benefit or survival.

Ignoring clients' needs, Shady Agents push bad deals forward with the aim of forcing a party to capitulate ensuring the property closes and the agent gets paid. This is common when there is an unqualified buyer, a low bank appraisal or an unresolved home-inspection issue. Invariably an agent's high-pressure tactics will anger one or more parties to the transaction. Now you know why Shady Agents seldom attend closings.

Unethical Behavior Is Expected and Tolerated

The dubious reputation of real estate agents precedes them, so consumers expect a degree of chicanery. Complaints are filed but many go unreported because consumers don't have the time or know-how to exact justice. To learn how, see chapters 41 and 42.

Consumers Are Willing Accomplices

Dishonest sellers will list with a Shady Agent who agrees to conceal a defect in their property. This is often accomplished by listing with an agent who is a family member or family friend. Conspiracies are very difficult to detect and defeat.

Lack of Real Estate Education

Defenders of the status quo argue most agents are honest and those that are not merely lack education because the educational requirements to obtain a license are minimal. Applicants need only a high school diploma to attend a 50–150-hour course and pass a state exam that takes about an hour. The Florida Department of Business and Professional Regulation website demonstrates their minimalist approach to real estate licensing this way:

> "Examinations play a vital role in the credentialing process—assuring minimal competence to practice a profession at the entry level."

Lack of Ethics Training

As of 2011, only six states require ethics training as part of their licensing requirements: California, Georgia, Iowa, Oklahoma, Ohio, and New Jersey. Note that New Jersey's real estate license educational requirement is a high school diploma and a seventy-five-hour real estate course. In comparison, the state's requirement for a hairstylist license is 1,200 hours!

States without any ethics training requirements rely on the National Association of Realtors' (NAR) Quadrennial online training course. The NAR trade group requires its dues-paying members to take the course once every four years. The ninety-minute course includes a review of NAR's Code of Ethics and Standards of Practice.

Agent Training Focused on Making Money

The state licensing course is the only real estate education most agents receive. An agent's firm may offer training but they focus on selling techniques, i.e., how to make money. The training includes:

- ✓ Goal setting

- ✓ Lead generation

✓ Converting FSBOs to exclusive listings

✓ Dealing with objections—when the customer says no

✓ Closing the sale.

Training sessions may include a pep rally, where a top agent guest lectures the class about the big money to be made selling real estate. Again, real estate law and ethical practice is ignored because the training is not designed to enhance an agent's knowledge of licensing laws. Instead, it emphasizes the psychology of consumer behavior with the aim of producing motivated sales agents with a "sell it now" geared to make money.

Sales Awards Based on Income

Many sellers assume so-called "Top Agents" are the best qualified to handle the sale of their home. They never consider the unethical tactics some Top Agents use to close their sales. Be warned, a study showed high-income agents are more likely to bend the rules.[2]

Unsupervised Independent Contractors

Tax and insurance regulations classify real estate agents as "independent contractors" because firms only control agents as to how their commissions are split and not how they conduct business. Even though broker/owners are legally tasked with supervising their agents, firms encourage agents to work independently from home, where oversight is nonexistent. The lack of an authority figure in a commission-only enterprise of independent contractors naturally leads to unethical business practices.

Government Authority is Out of Sight and Out of Mind

The only interaction an agent has with the government licensing agency is when applying for the license and after a consumer files a complaint. The Walmart greeter says hello as a means of deterring theft.

Lack of Fidelity

Licensing law provides that agents have a fiduciary obligation to their clients including reasonable care, undivided loyalty, confidentiality, and full disclosure. This includes working to obtain the highest and best price for your property. Remember this when your agent pressures you for your "bottom-line price."

---

[2] *Ethics in Real Estate,* edited by Stephen E. Roulac, Volume 5, Chapter 13; *An Empirical Analysis of Real Estate Brokerage Ethics,* by A. Ason Okoruwa and A. Frank Thompson, pg. 269. The Howard Hughes Company and the American Real Estate Society.

Cadre of Accomplices

Shady Agents have symbiotic relationships with lawyers, mortgage brokers, exterminators, home inspectors, landscapers, contractors, and each other. Agents are required to disclose if they receive a fee when referring such professionals to their clients. But even without kickbacks, the group effect creates a situational quid pro quo with all working for the common goal of closing the deal and getting paid.

✓ Lender provides a favorable loan prequalification letter.

✓ Home inspector exaggerates or minimizes a problem.

✓ Attorney tweaks the contract to insure the transaction closes.

✓ Contractor exaggerates or minimizes the cost of repairs.

✓ Listing and selling agents reveal their clients' negotiating positions.

3
CHAPTER

Common Home-Selling Myths

Sellers with preconceived and naïve notions about how real estate is sold may resort to burying statutes of St. Joseph in their yards. But hope is not a strategy. Follows are 4 other common home selling myths created down here on earth.

<u>Advertising Sells Houses</u>

The National Association of Realtor's "2010 Profile of Home Buyers and Sellers" survey showed only 2 percent of buyers found the home they purchased through a newspaper advertisement. Despite that fact, agents will hype the value of advertising to justify their commission.

Sellers should ignore that hype and focus on preparing their home, pricing it properly and selecting an honest and capable agent. Sellers having trouble selling usually spend too much time worrying how their home is marketed in a newspaper or on some heavily promoted website like Zillow.

Your Listing Agent Will Sell Your Home

The common assumption that your listing agent will deliver the buyer for your home was shown to be false in the 2005 Turnbull and Dumbrow study, "Identifying Agent Specific Influences in the Brokerage Process." The study showed only about 17 percent of houses are listed and sold by the same agent. More importantly, the study also showed sellers received a lower sales price when the home was sold by the listing agent. Most sellers find that a listing agent with his/her own offer tend to be an advocate for the buyer.

You Need a Big Company with Presence

The idea that large branded firms with many offices, agents, and listings have the best chance of finding buyers willing to pay the highest price. Nervous sellers naturally find security in numbers. But the Turnbull and Dumbrow study found that the size of the firm is inconsequential: "There is no evidence of pervasive performance advantages for larger firms…for either listing or selling functions." Again, your agent is more important than the firm.

Paying a High Commission Will Attract More Agents

Offering agents a commission higher than what the majority of other sellers are paying will *not* induce more showings. Agents only show homes they expect their customers to buy. They will not risk losing the confidence of their buyers by trying to sell them a property they do not want. Shady Agents can show buyers a home they do not want, but they can only convince them to buy it by using deceit.

4

CHAPTER

The Simplistic Selling Plan and Where Buyers Come From

It's All about Perceptions

What sellers and inexperienced agents know about selling real estate has been learned by watching how consumer goods are marketed or promoted in the media. Ergo, they naïvely assume advertising is primarily responsible for attracting buyers and selling homes. It follows that prospective listing agents will happily agree with that assumption as a means to getting a seller to sign their listing contract. Here's the typical simplistic marketing plan advertised by a large, nationally branded firm:

"... [We] will create a marketing plan for your home that will help distinguish it in your local marketplace and attract buyers to your property. This may include advertising in the newspaper, posting your listing on the Internet, holding an open house, and more."

Agents who focus exclusively on marketing will advertise your home and hold Open Houses while you both wait for a buyer to appear. When that produces nothing, most agents will then begin hinting (so as not to insult you) that your asking price must be reduced. This is why Shady Agents push for long-term, unbreakable listing contracts.

Where Buyers Come From

The NAR's "2010 Profile of Home Buyers and Sellers" reported 38% of buyers were introduced to the home they bought through an Internet site like Realtor.com. 37% were introduced to the home by an agent member of MLS. Yard signs garnered 11%; friends 6%; homebuilders 4%. Only 2% found their home through advertising.

The majority of buyers search the Realtor.com database to preselect homes and then use a friend or relative with a real estate license to see them.

5
CHAPTER

Preparing Your Home for Sale

Money Finds Good Investments

Sellers who do little to improve their home's appearance fail to realize other sellers are competing against them for buyers by improving the condition of their homes. Buyers seek homes in top-notch condition the same way money finds good investments.

When your home is not in near-perfect condition, the only way to compete with those that are is to reduce your price. To avoid that, make the needed improvements *before* selecting an agent and listing in MLS. Don't put off repairs by assuming buyers want to redo a home the way that they want it. They don't. Buyers who make offers on homes needing repair always exaggerate the cost and deduct it from their offer. This is why new homes are easy to sell. Buyers know there is absolutely nothing to do but move in.

One sure way to get your home looking new is to replace or update your kitchen and baths. If that's not in the budget, then at least get rid of clutter, because it distracts buyers. Empty your closets by donating clothes you never wear to the Salvation Army. Avoid

renting a storage container that remains in your driveway because it will remind buyers you have little storage space. Better to rent a dumpster and throw it all away.

Depersonalize the Home

Agents and their nosey buyers will look in your closets and at family photos to learn about you and why you are selling. For example, a home with lots of children's toys but devoid of any men's clothing points to a divorce. Such perceptions, whether real or imagined, lead agents and their buyers to assume you have no choice but to entertain lowball offers. You cannot do much about prying eyes except to depersonalize the home by removing family photos and memorabilia.

Instruct Buyers to Their Remove Shoes

To convey a message that their home is in near-perfect condition, some sellers post a "Please Remove Shoes" sign at the front door. Of course, this is a joke when the home and floors are a mess.

Turn On the Lights

When possible, turn on the lights when your home is being shown because bright homes show better than dark ones. When you leave the house for the day, leave some lights on and open closed blinds.

"Houseatosis"

If you regularly cook with oil and spices like garlic and your stove is not vented to the outside, your home probably smells like what you eat. Cooking odors distract buyers. You cannot smell the odor because you are used to it.

Pet Pee Will Reduce Your Home's Value

Attempting to mask the odor of pet urine with scented candles, plug-in fragrances, or by leaving windows open (in the dead of winter) will not fool many buyers. Hoping you will sell your home to another pet lover who will overlook the stink and the stained floors is a pipe dream. Most homes for sale do not smell like dog and cat pee. If you do not eliminate the odor, you will be forced to reduce your price.

If you have a barking dog that likes to jump on people, do not introduce it to buyers hoping to calm it down. This will only highlight the fact you have an uncontrollable pet and involve you in an unnecessary conversation with the buyers. Warning prospective buyers your dog "only bites when it's scared" will distract them from looking at your house. Take your dog outside. Do not put a pet in a room with a sign that reads, *"DO NOT OPEN—DOG,"* rest assured that buyers will not open the door and they will not see the room.

6
CHAPTER

Beat the Inspectors: Fix Your Home First

Your listing agent should identify cosmetic and home-inspection problems with your property before listing it in MLS. Do not ignore problems thinking it's better to wait and see if potential buyers find them. When discovered, buyers may assume you are hiding other problems. Most buyers exaggerate the cost of repairs and will seek to deduct that amount from the purchase price. You and your agent will find it nearly impossible to convince them their estimates are too high.

Skeptical buyers will bring a trusted third party to evaluate a suspected problem *before* making an offer. This is often a relative or family friend with or without construction experience who assumes the role of protector and overstates the cost and extent of remediation. The most critical home inspector is the father of a buyer, especially if the buyer is a daughter. In real estate circles, fathers are known as the "kiss of death," as they find problems with all homes.

A problem discovered by a home inspection may hinder a future sale if your current buyer terminates the contract. Once a defect is revealed, your listing agent has a legal obligation to disclose the defect to all future buyers and buyer agents—even if the item has been repaired! To avoid this nightmare, **make repairs prior to meeting with any agent to list your home.** If you are uncertain where to look for problems, pay a home inspector to inspect your home *before* you meet with an agent to list it for sale. Here are a few common problems that will threaten a sale:

✓ Faulty septic system or sewer line

✓ Old and rusty HVAC

✓ Horizontal cracks on foundation wall

✓ Improper footings under foundation wall

✓ No footings under lally columns

✓ Leaking oil tank

✓ Roof with missing shingles

✓ Black mold anywhere

✓ Aluminum wiring

✓ Contaminated drinking water.

And don't even think of adding a remark to your MLS data sheet offering a monetary credit for structural or cosmetic defects in your home. The comment will only highlight the problem to buyers and their home inspectors.

(AGENT SELECTION PHASE)

7
CHAPTER

How to Interview Prospective Listing Agents

To get a good read on a prospective agent's character, you and your significant other should interview the agent together. Be warned, the agent is also interviewing you to determine how motivated you are to sell, i.e., lower your price. Resist the urge to talk. Agents will reveal a lot about themselves and what they know about selling real estate if you let them talk. If the agent is nervous, it probably means the agent rarely lists houses. Most agents prefer to show homes, because a listing contract makes them obligated to accomplish something.

Many states require that agents immediately explain the laws of agency upon meeting with you for the first time. Not performing this task does not necessarily make the agent dishonest, though it demonstrates the agent's laziness or ignorance of the law. (See Chapter 10, "The Law of Agency.")

Perform a quick integrity test and ask the agent for a copy of her/his real estate license. Note the agent's demeanor in response to this request as it may reveal something about the agent's character.

Ask what fee or commission the agent charges. The agent should have a simple and definitive answer. Be wary of agents who seem confused or insulted by the question. Dismiss any agent who claims commissions are set by custom or some authority. (See Chapter 12, "How to Discount the Commission.")

Never discuss personal or financial problems causing you to sell unless you are in the midst of a foreclosure. Revealing problems may get you needed sympathy, but agents will *always* use that information against you during contract negotiations. Never divulge the balance of the loan(s) against your property. Never discuss a "bottom-line" price with any agent. Be very leery of agents who ask for this number. Do not make one up because the number you give will eventually trap you. Tell agents you expect "market value."

Most agents will say things like: "I love your home's natural color" or "The granite countertops match the maple cabinets beautifully." Agents will flatter you to get your listing, but it is more important to hear the negative things the agent believes may hinder the sale or raise home-inspection issues. Regrettably, most agents will not say anything negative until you have signed a listing contract.

While touring your home, an agent will try to decipher how serious you are about getting top dollar. If you go from room to room turning on lights and apologizing for your home's condition, the agent will naturally assume you are more concerned about getting it sold than receiving top dollar. The agent will then handle the listing and any subsequent offers with that in mind. Better to show agents how serious you are about success by completing improvements and/or repairs before they see your home.

Most states require agents to inspect and confirm that the systems in your home are in working order, e.g., the HVAC, electric, and plumbing. Think twice about listing with an agent who does not ask about them but immediately pressures you to sign the listing contract. An honest agent will take the time to discuss items essential to a successful sale such as:

✓ Do you plan to open and clean the pool?

✓ Are you including personal property like the washer/dryer?

✓ What will you do with the dog during showings?

✓ Will you replace the stained carpet before listing in MLS?

✓ Will the broken lights in your basement be repaired?

✓ How will the house be shown?

✓ Will you be using a lockbox?

✓ Will your boat remain in the driveway?

✓ Will the front door be repaired to close properly?

✓ What will you do about the damp basement?

✓ Will redecorating be completed before listing in MLS?

✓ How will negotiations be handled?

CHAPTER 7

Ask agents what they will do to sell homes. Listen very carefully to what they say. Dismiss agents who have little to say or make promises about what their firm will do, e.g., posting your home to the company website, advertising, and holding open houses. Some sellers are persuaded by these promises because they assume that's how homes are sold. A detailed list of an agent's selling responsibilities can be found in Chapter 13, "The Tricks and Traps of the Listing Contract."

Before the agent leaves, ask for all documents that you will be required to sign if you list with the agent. You must have time to read and understand the documents before being pressured to sign them.

8
CHAPTER

What to Look for in a Listing Agent

Above all else, selecting a knowledgeable, honest and experienced agent with impeccable character is the most important thing needed to sell your home. The trick is to find one. Licensing authorities require applicants to possess good character, trustworthiness, honesty, and integrity. The licensee vetting process includes asking applicants if they have ever been convicted of crimes like forgery, burglary, robbery, theft, or criminal conspiracy to defraud. Authorities will revoke a license if the answer is later found to be false. But since criminal records are rarely cross-checked, agents can sell for years before an infraction causes an investigation revealing a previous conviction. Here is a disciplinary action published by the NJ Real Estate Commission:

"…the Commission revoked Mr. Maia's license and imposed a $500 fine for misrepresentation, unworthiness, dishonesty or bad faith, being convicted of a crime, knowledge of which the Commission did not have…Mr. Maia failed to disclose prior criminal convictions on his application for a real estate license."

Calling a large and heavily promoted firm and listing your home with the first agent that answers the phone is a mistake. Lazy agents hang around offices to socialize because they have no customers, clients or business. You can do better.

The NAR reports 41 percent of sellers selected their listing agent after asking a friend who has recently sold a home for a recommendation. This is a good idea, but it is important that you interview and compare at least one or two other agents.

Get a good read on an agent's character and business practice by listening to what the agent promises to do *after* uploading your home to MLS. Eliminate agents who have nothing more than a scripted presentation about how great their company is. These agents practice the simplistic selling plan discussed in Chapter 4 and will do little once you sign their unbreakable listing contract.

Keep in mind that agents are in sales, so have a healthy skepticism about boastful claims of past achievements. Perform due diligence and ask for copies of the agent's current and sold listings.

Select an Agent Who Primarily Lists Houses

A nationally syndicated columnist once wrote the best way to select a listing agent is to call a local brokerage and ask for the firm's top agent. But listing your home with a so-called "Top Agent" may be troublesome, especially if the agent works primarily with buyers. If you want a top agent, you should interview the firm's top *listing agent* because according to the Turnbull and Dumbrow study, "Agents who specialize more heavily in listing functions obtain higher prices. Agents who specialize more heavily in selling [showing homes] appear to enhance buyer bargaining power…leading to lower selling prices."

Consider the Agent's Listing Experience

List with an agent who has had at least three listings sell in the past 12 months. Ask for copies of those listings. If the agent includes the listings of his/her firm's other agents, ignore them because those agents will not be working for you. Review the listings to be sure the agent does a good job posting all the information about the property. Are there many missing spaces? Are the room sizes and current taxes listed? Is the photo of the home adequate? (See Chapter 15, "How Your Home Appears In MLS—The Data Sheet.")

A Good Agent Puts Promises in Writing

The listing contract only obligates your agent to upload your home to MLS. There is absolutely nothing written about the promises the agent verbally made. This is another reason why many agents do little once your home has been listed. Good agents will provide a written list enumerating all they will do to sell your home. This is detailed in Chapter 13, "The Tricks and Traps of the Listing Contract."

Select an Agent You Can Manage

While your home is listed in MLS, your job will be to confirm your agent performs the written list of responsibilities that were included with the listing agreement (See Chapter 13, "The Tricks and Traps of the Listing Contract"). Some sellers who list with so-called "Top Agents" are afraid to question them about what they do. I suspect they were duped by the hype and/or blinded by the "Top Agent" status. To effectively manage an agent, you must:

✓ Maintain a relationship of mutual respect.

✓ Be demanding but never ungrateful.

✓ Communicate with the agent on a regular basis.

✓ Be involved in all decisions throughout the process.

✓ Respect your agent's experience but ask what is happening.

✓ The relationship must be a win-win proposition.

✓ Your agent must discuss problems without fearing retribution.

✓ Monitor the list of your agent's responsibilities outlined on the listing contract.

Your Agent Must Know How to Qualify Buyers

Ask prospective agents how they qualify buyers for a mortgage loan. Ask agents to explain the difference between conventional and a FHA loan. Agents who say they let the lender "figure all that stuff out" do not know how to qualify buyers and will have trouble with other basic concepts and responsibilities.

Your Agent Must Be a Problem Solver

Your agent's emotional maturity and skill in anticipating and solving disputes among the parties may save a transaction heading for disaster. Your agent must have the professional know-how to quickly resolve common problems that threaten transactions:

✓ Days before the closing the buyers discover the condominium association is charging owners a "special assessment" of $10,000 for new roofs, and they refuse to close.

✓ The buyers' lender will not commit to the loan because the appraiser claims one bedroom is not a "legal" because it has no closet.

Consider the Agent's People Skills

Selling real estate is a people business and although transactions appear similar, they are as different as the personalities of the parties involved. Mixed among the contract legalese, poorly written deeds, and complex loan programs are the motives of the buyers, sellers, lawyers, mortgage brokers, appraisers, title companies, home inspectors, contractors, exterminators, and local government officials.

Think about a prospective agent's ability to recognize and control a dishonest party who purposely creates problems with the aim of renegotiating the contract or backing out of the deal at your expense.

Your Agent Must Be Able to Work with Competing Agents

Some agents have adolescent jealousies of competing agents that may impede the creation of a sale or destroy one out of spite. This is often revealed when an agent complains too loudly about another agent's actions or appearance.

For example, a buyers' agent may need documentation confirming your property is not in a flood zone. If your listing agent refuses to deliver the needed flood map to the other agent, the sale may be lost. Then, when you ask, "What happened to those buyers?" your agent will probably respond, "The other agent wouldn't do her job, and now they're gone."

Your Agent Must Follow Up

After an offer has been signed by all parties, the resulting contract will take on a life of its own. Without constant guidance from your agent, the sale can be lost or the closing postponed. Your agent is responsible for managing the contract contingencies and confirming each step of the process with you. Here are a few examples of what you will need to ask your agent:

✓ Do we have a bona fide contract signed by all parties?

✓ Do the buyers know the lawn tractor (or similar) is not included in the sale?

✓ Are the buyers using a lawyer?

✓ Do all parties have a copy of the contract?

✓ Have the buyers made their required escrow deposit?

✓ Who is holding the buyers' escrow money? Where is that money?

✓ Have the buyers applied for their loan?

✓ Did the lender's appraiser get in the house?

✓ Did the home appraise for the contract price?

✓ Have the home-inspection issues been resolved—in writing?

✓ Do we have a solid contract?

✓ Has the buyers' home sold? When will it close?

✓ Do we have the certificate of occupancy needed to close?

✓ Are the buyers on track to close on time?

✓ Is there anything that will prevent the home from closing on time?

Check the Agent's Complaint History

Convicted felons are not permitted to obtain a real estate license, though many lie about their criminal record to obtain one. Before working with an agent, check with your state's licensing agency to see if the licensee has ever been disciplined. Google the agent's name and firm for complaints or lawsuits. See Chapter 42 for a contact list of real estate licensing authorities.

Common Traits of a Good Agent

✓ Acts like a social worker – empathizes with clients problems

✓ Feels a moral obligation to help people

✓ Has patience to obtain highest possible price

✓ Builds relationships

✓ Is enthusiastic and positive

✓ Believes money is a reward for doing good work

✓ Provides a breakable listing contract

✓ Protects and promotes his clients' interests

✓ Has at least one year of experience

✓ Has at least three current listings

✓ Accepts responsibilities—including those of co-agents

✓ Accepts responsibility when things go wrong

✓ Is a problem solver and does not play the blame game

✓ Can successfully handle a crisis

✓ Finds it difficult to lie

✓ Lives by the Golden Rule

✓ Has integrity, believing honesty is the best policy

✓ Will never pressure you to sign anything

✓ Is an active listener

✓ Does the right thing, even when no one is looking

✓ Communicates with clients on a regular basis

✓ Healthy and energetic—able to work nights and weekends

✓ Dependable—does not neglect phone calls or appointments

✓ Has completed additional real estate-related education

✓ Holds your hand throughout the process

✓ Controls his/her ego to remain focused on doing the right thing

✓ Warns of bad deals despite losing a commission

✓ Tells it like it is, even when the solution is worse than the problem

✓ Is female. The Okoruwa and Thompson study showed that female agents are less likely to "bend the rules."

9
CHAPTER

Shady Agent Personalities and Proclivities

<u>Top Agents—The Devil's Bargain</u>

Sellers employing ambitious "Top Agents" are oblivious to the tactics some of these agents use to close their deals. Ultimately, when an offer arrives and negotiations begin, many sellers complain their "Top Agent" seems to be working for the buyers!

There are two types of top agents: those who work hard and receive repeat business and referrals from satisfied customers and those that are less trustworthy. In "An Empirical Analysis of Real Estate Brokerage Ethics," Ason Okuruwa and Frank Thompson wrote, "It appears the higher the income level, the more likely it is an agent will bend the rules to close a deal."

"Top Agent" monikers are used to validate an agent's probable success in selling your home. This is why agents promote their awards in the local paper, on their website, business cards, lawn signs, e-mails, and on the brochures of your home. Here are other impressive-sounding sales-awards:

- ✓ Million Dollar Sales Club

- ✓ The President's Circle

- ✓ Multimillion Dollar Sales Club

- ✓ The Circle of Excellence

- ✓ Ambassadors Club

Sales awards based on the number of sales or sales volume are not a measure of an agent's honesty and should be taken with a grain of salt. No independent authority verifies the sales volume needed for membership in any sales club. Although the Realtor® trade group claims its "applications are audited for accuracy and compliance to established criteria," the agent's broker or office manager signs off on the transactions listed on their agent's application. The top agents are then used by the firm as a propaganda tool to recruit other agents who at times believe the grass is always greener on the other side.

To qualify for top-agent awards, some agents will take credit for sales made by another agent. In New Jersey, the end-of-year scramble to qualify for the Realtors Circle of Excellence Sales Award becomes so chaotic that the Garden State MLS prohibits agents from transferring sales credits thirty days prior to the application's due date. Note the MLS does nothing to stop the dishonesty.

Enter "The Dragon Lady"

The Dragon Lady is an aggressive Top Agent frustrated by her perception that other agents impede her success. She justifies her notorious belligerence by calling it "no-nonsense professionalism" and portrays herself as a "closer." Sellers who mistake her hubris for an assertive selling style foolishly list with her thinking, "She's a son of a bitch, but she's our son of a bitch." What they don't know is that the Dragon Lady is despised by other agents because she operates her business as a zero-sum game. She's been known to remove or knock down competitors' For Sale signs and/or steal other agents' customers.

The Dragon Lady is a know-it-all who insists on controlling everything including the sale of your home. At first, the screening of other agents' buyers seems professional, but her modus operandi is to prevent other agents from showing your home so she can sell it herself and collect the entire commission. She purposely omits your name and phone number from the MLS data sheet and includes: "Do not contact sellers—all appointments and communications through listing agent." But when buyer agents call, they get nothing but voicemail. If the Dragon Lady returns the call, she is uncooperative and downright nasty, demanding the appointment be made 24 hours in advance.

When another agent has an offer for your home, The Dragon Lady will delay the offer by demanding to see the buyers' mortgage commitment, knowing no buyer can obtain a commitment until an executed contract exists. So after many angry calls from the buyers' agent, the Dragon Lady relents—with conditions. She will accept a prequalification letter if accompanied by a bank statement proving the buyers' source of funds. Other times The Dragon Lady demands to speak directly with the buyers' lender to confirm the authenticity of the prequalification letter. This dog and pony show goes on behind her clients' backs. Agents who have tangled with the Dragon Lady avoid showing her listings. Did I mention the Dragon Lady never offers a breakable listing contract?

The Slick Shyster

Any jerk with a brain knows an intimidating personality is a necessity for top agents like me. When working with buyers, I show three homes and then pressure them to buy one—implying that out of all the homes in MLS, there are no others to consider. The tactic works and I've got plenty of Top Agent awards and this bestselling book to prove it.

Jealous competitors say I badger people beyond the point of being rude. That's an exaggeration. But if I find a comfortable chair, I won't leave a home until somebody signs my contract. Truth be told -- I get the job done. When clients complain I ask them, "Do you want me to sell your house or what"?

My written market analysis of a home lists comparable properties that match its architectural style and room count, but I purposely omit square footage enabling me to manipulate its estimated value. Sometimes I want a high number, other times I want it low. When clients question my calculations I tell them a property is only worth what somebody's willing to pay for it. That usually shuts them up.

Anything I do to sell a client's home is a Machiavellian favor to be repaid another time. For example, when a listing contract is about to expire I'll complain I spent a lot of money printing property brochures and demand the home must be relisted with me because of all the money I spent.

I avoid responsibility by insinuating whatever's needed to sell a house is the sellers' problem. I like to keep sellers on edge with annoying questions like, "Have any agents shown the house yet?" or "Where's that copy of your deed I asked for?"

When there's a problem. I never offer options; only ultimatums such as, "Here's what you need to do now."

I may not know everything about real estate law, but when it comes to spewing baloney, I'm the best. I invent laws to suit me. For example, if a client asks me to handle a smoke detector inspection I'll claim laws prohibit me from representing homeowners at municipal inspections.

I take control by talking fast and hurrying the transaction so the outcome benefits me. While sellers are about to reject a low offer, I will push a pen in their hand and insist they must first sign the contract to "legally acknowledge their rejection." It makes them think twice before saying no.

I call at odd hours to give the impression I'm always working. I keep sold property listed in MLS and keep SOLD signs on unlisted property to collect the names and phone numbers of the buyers (suckers) who call. I push sellers to hold purchase money mortgages for unqualified buyers. I call it "creative financing".

When a sale goes bad, I don't return deposit money until threatened with legal action. I then negotiate to keep some of the money for my time and effort.

The best way to handle me is to keep your distance. Befriending me is a mistake because I'm all business all the time. I don't need any friends. If you must confront me, be firm and remain calm, because I thrive on conflict. My favorite slogan is, "good guys finish last."

Country Clubbers

I once re-listed a home of a PhD who programmed missile guidance systems for the military. This well-educated seller had previously listed with a firm that had a large brass chandelier conspicuously displayed in their office window. He expected his well-dressed agent would have plenty of wealthy buyers because she was a member of the local country club. But after he signed her listing contract, he never saw her again.

Country Club agents have little motivation to work because their spouses support them. They avoid menial tasks because they customarily pay someone to do that work for them. They dread breaking a fingernail installing a lockbox or yard sign, will not venture into basements for fear of spiders and will not be caught dead at a septic inspection.

Country Clubbers may be duplicitous when negotiating because they are suckers for referent power. They switch loyalties when they perceive the other party having wealth, power, or celebrity status. Remember those high-school cliques? Nothing has changed.

You may like their professional demeanor but know that when a problem arises, Country Clubbers extend no special favors. You will be treated in a businesslike manner, insuring the deal closes and the Country Clubber gets paid. After all, country-club memberships are very expensive.

On the other hand, there are exceptions. Some Country Clubbers are diligent and hardworking because they compete with a successful spouse for success. They enjoy repeat business and have enviable reputations for handling the majority of home sales in well-to-do neighborhoods.

The Team

A team of three or more agents are assembled to do the leader's grunt work. One prepares brochures and mailers, another completes the MLS input forms and answers the phone, while another installs the lawn sign and lockbox and follows up on showings. Team members are paid a stipend or portion of each sale.

Teams use the bandwagon effect to obtain listings, boasting their success with an advertising catch-phrase like: "Why have just one agent when you can have a whole team working for you?" Though

you are led to believe the team provides better service, the concept was concocted for the sole purpose of generating more income for the team leader. The team leader's job is to get your signature on the listing contract or on a contract of sale. Teams don't have listings; they have accounts. There's a difference.

Be certain the team leader knows you are holding him/her ultimately responsible for the sale of your property. You should have the team leader's personal cell and/or home phone to prevent the hassle of getting secondhand information from a team member. Be warned, team leaders often have two cell phones: one they answer and another that is automatically sent to voicemail.

Spouses That Sell Houses

When spouses sell houses, the husband is usually the macho negotiator and closer who does the heavy lifting such as measuring rooms, taking photographs, and installing the lawn sign and lockbox. The wife often plays the "good soldier," preparing brochures and communicating between you, her cantankerous husband, and other agents. One spouse may have another real estate-related job such as appraising or lending. If you enjoy watching the everyday dynamics of another couple's relationship, then listing with this dynamic duo may be interesting and fun.

Corporate Loafers

Many victims of corporate downsizing find refuge working for large real estate companies with similar corporate atmospheres. These agents wear a company name tag to create the perception they are competent professionals from a large successful company.

Guilty of corporate loafing and prone to self-pity, these agents frequent broker open houses where they enjoy coffee, cake, and stimulating conversation. They have a mind-set that the company is responsible for everything—including the sale of your home. They follow the simplistic selling plan outlined in Chapter 4 because they lack basic selling skills and get mired in the minutiae of contracts, zoning regulations, and real estate law.

Corporate Loafers are only available during standard office hours and avoid working weekends. Selling real estate is usually a stop-gap measure to pay the bills until they find another job or a spouse retires and begins collecting a pension or social security. The good news is they are pleasant, reliable, honest, and usually get help from a reliable source when solving a problem.

Old Timers

Old agents in poor health will avoid the tasks necessary to sell your home. They will not have the energy to measure rooms or visit the tax assessor's office to confirm your home's square footage. Instead, they will rely on dubious measurements found on an old listing or brochure. They will put off installing the For Sale sign or reinstalling it when blows over in a storm. Agents who find it difficult to negotiate attic or basement stairs will have little firsthand knowledge about your home. When you ask for feedback on a showing, they say they will call you back, but they never do.

Old Timers stop working at five o'clock because by 7:00 p.m. they are semi-conscious on a couch watching reruns of "Dancing With the Stars". They never work weekends and cancel appointments when they hear rumors of rain or snow. Agents in poor health and lacking energy should not be selling real estate.

The Burned-Out Broker

This broker once operated his own brokerage and has been selling real estate for over 25 years. During one of the many economic downturns, he lost his passion and the ability to inspire his agents to do the right thing. He began recruiting top agents by secretly offering them large commission splits. When his other agents found out, they felt betrayed and quit the firm forcing him to sell the firm to a competitor. To save his reputation he argued the sale was a merger designed to provide better service for his agents and clients.

Now working for the competitor, he has much experience but little patience with other agents who ask too many stupid questions. Lacking initiative, he only shows homes if the buyers have driven by them first. He's slow to return phone calls and refuses to work past 5:00 p.m. Not a fan of new technology, his property brochures are simplistic photocopies of the MLS data sheet. However, the old guy is handy and will install smoke detectors and make minor repairs to obtain needed certificates of occupancy. He doesn't have many buyers because his large gas-guzzling car smells like a lunchbox.

Loners

Loners are the quintessential independent contractors. They are confident and cocky and don't like to be told what to do. Selling real estate is a good fit for loners because they shun the authority in traditional employer/employee relationships. They may have a tremendous work ethic but they are rarely consistent big producers because of their poor people skills. In the workplace they are antagonistic, impatient, easily angered, and confrontational so their selling technique is usually the hard sell.

They tend to have strong black-and-white philosophies about right and wrong. When a sale is prematurely terminated, loners immediately blame the other agent and become vindictive. They have a long list of enemies and will exact retribution when they cross paths with the offending agent on another deal. However, some lonely loners can be extremely loyal and honest when secure in knowing they will collect a commission from you. Unfortunately, they expect a lifetime commitment on your part.

Loners have self-serving relationships and over time their social contacts dwindle leaving them without a stable support mechanism. Eventually they resort to selling land or commercial real estate where the transactions are all business and the parties are like minded lawyers or corporations.

Promoters

If you believe advertising sells houses and liked to be entertained, then list with a promoter. Promoters work for large branded firms and embrace the misconception that homes must be merchandised like soap. Promoters have vivacious personalities and may drive a car or truck with their name, face, and company logo wrapped all over. Some gain attention by wearing

an ostentatious hat or some other signature outfit. They give away boatloads of refrigerator magnets, calendars, note pads, and pens. Their name and logo are on your home's brochure, lawn sign, directional signs, and the balloons tied to open house signs.

Promoters claim their commission pays for advertising your home. But the promises of promotion are used to convince you to pay a 6 percent commission. At best, the promotion only serves the promoter and his/her endeavor to obtain other listings.

Some promoters are IT savvy and will crow about the thousands of hits your home received on their website. Although the number of views a property posted on the Internet receives is inconsequential, at least the promoter knows more about IT than most agents.

Unfortunately, most promoters are a one trick pony and subscribe to the simplistic selling plan discussed in Chapter 4. Once they upload your home to MLS, dazzle you with color flyers and run some ads, they consider their job complete. Should the home remain unsold, they can claim it wasn't anything they didn't do. Ultimately, they cannot offer much advice because promotion is their only forte.

Though you may be put off by their high energy and sometimes quirky personalities, they mean no harm. Promoters are usually honest because their income depends on referrals from past customers and clients and they know it is easier to maintain a reputation than to repair one.

Newbies

Fresh out of sales training and ready for business with the latest smartphone, new agents spend more time designing their business cards than prospecting for customers. Their lack of a customer base leaves them with little income.

Newbies rarely list homes because they have yet to understand how homes are sold and where buyers come from. Hence, they follow the simplistic selling plan outlined in Chapter 4. They have no alternative but to work with buyers, chauffeuring them from house to house in hopes they stumble upon one they like.

Experienced agents take advantage of newbies by convincing them to sit their open houses promising they can keep the names and phone numbers of the looky-loos who show up. A sympathetic agent may take a new agent under his or her wing, but many of these mentors then demand a piece of every commission the newbie earns.

The Busybody Soccer Mom

The Busybody Soccer Mom is a parasitic agent that generates leads from her neighborhood, where she sends promotional trinkets like refrigerator magnets with her photo and the tagline: "Greenfield Acres #1 Listing Agent."

She is a nosey gadabout who is the first to list neighborhood homes of those who die. Her name and photo are on supermarket shopping carts. While at her kid's soccer game she wears her company name tag and connects with neighbors to tell them how much a friend's house sold for. She follows up those chats by sending invites to her Facebook page, where she posts information about here real estate deals and her other multilevel marketing business.

When she learns you're thinking of selling, the Busybody becomes your new best friend. In the event you list with another agent, she will literally flip out and accuse you of depriving her kids of a private school education.

Should you list with this agent, you'll learn she's an expert on everything. Without asking, she will rearrange your family room furniture to create what she calls "a better presentation." The Busybody Soccer Mom has no capacity to listen because she never shuts up. She's a part-time agent who markets property based on the simplistic selling plan outlined in Chapter 4.

Incompetent Drama Queens

Drama Queens lead a stressful and sleepless life. They are products of a chaotic past that manifests as a debilitating anxiety where simple tasks become operatic calamities. Chronic stress degenerates the brain's nuerocircuitry and clouds the agent's comprehension of basic real estate concepts, e.g., the difference between an offer and a contract or a mortgage and a promissory note. Easily overwhelmed when wrecked with worry and self-doubt, they will forget to tell you about a pending offer. When they miss deadlines and appointments, they use dramatic excuses, e.g., "My cat was having kittens!" Sometimes they create and enjoy drama because it allows them to commiserate with others.

Drama Queens are ineffective negotiators because conflict exacerbates their anxiety and prevents them from developing a strategy to get from point A to point B. They talk too much causing their customers and clients to lose confidence. They show homes to the same unqualified buyer for years without making a sale because they cannot grasp the nuance between the buyer's real and false objections.

Drama Queens may be kooky and socially awkward. Rarely dressed for business, they may arrive at your home in a sweat suit—weather permitting. Their voicemail cannot receive messages because it's always full. They have trouble following directions to a home and need their buyers help to operate a GPS. They fumble opening lockboxes and unlocking doors. While backing out of your driveway, they may accidentally run over your mailbox.

When a transaction goes bad, they feign ignorance and face the possibility of being charged by the licensing authorities with incompetence.

Greedy Agents

Greedy Agents are short-term thinkers obsessed with the stuff money can buy. Desperate to preserve their self-esteem and reputations as top producers, they live stressful lives on the brink of financial disaster. Greedy agents usually come from modest backgrounds and after making a couple of big sales, they spend like crazy. They buy trendy consumer items rationalizing that anything used in business is tax deductible and will make them more productive. Unfortunately, they must frequently upgrade their latest gadget because the one they have never seems to make them more money.

When the economy sours, their ethical decisions and command of the facts are tainted by their struggle to pay the bills. Always telling dunning creditors, "The check is in the mail," they find it easy to lie.

To conceal their anxiety, Greedy Agents project a phony positive attitude about the market. When asked about market conditions, they cheerfully respond using obtuse quantitative statistics: "My dollar volume is up 12 percent over the same quarter last year", or "Offers on my listings have increased 22 percent!" Subconsciously they doubt their professional competency, so when they don't have an answer, they make one up.

Greedy Agents like to work with naïve first-time buyers and low-income subprime borrowers because they know how to convince them to buy homes with little or no money down. After all, they've been there and done that. They get deals done by pushing parties to sign and close before the scheduled date to satisfy an overdue credit card or tax lien.

Greedy Agents excuse their slipshod business practices under the guise of working too hard. "I'm very busy right now" is a standard response. Subsequently, most clients are relatives or friends of relatives because past customers will not recommend the Greedy Agent.

Financial stress takes its toll on Greedy Agents. Many get divorced and/or develop health problems. Happy Hour may become a daily event making communicating with them after 7 p.m. an adventure.

As they get older they beg for business by hinting they need money to pay for a medical procedure. When a customer falls for this ruse, they suddenly find religion and thank them with a sanctimonious, "May God bless you!" Listing with a Greedy Agent is another good reason to have a breakable listing contract.

(LISTING PHASE)

10
CHAPTER

The Law of Agency

Licensing law requires agents to disclose if they are working for the seller, the buyer, both buyer and seller, or just themselves. Agents are legally obligated to explain this before you divulge financial information that would give another party an unfair advantage.

No matter who an agent claims to represent, an agent's default position is to do what is best for them. Knowing that, license law dictates agents must declare one of the following types of agency:

✓ **Buyer agents** represent and owe their loyalty and fiduciary responsibility to the buyer. A buyer agent works to get the buyer the best deal, even if the seller is paying the commission.

✓ **Seller agents** represent and owe their loyalty and fiduciary responsibility to the seller, even when the sellers' agent produces the buyer for the home.

✓ **Disclosed dual agents** owe their loyalty and fiduciary responsibility to *both* the buyer and seller. Dual agency is the choice of most agents; they know consumers will agree to it because it seems fair. But fairness is impossible when an agent represents both parties. Note that Colorado, Florida, and Kansas prohibit dual agency.

✓ **Designated agency is** used when the firm you have listed your home with has the buyer. Your listing agent then becomes the "designated agent" representing you while another agent from the same firm represents the buyer. This arrangement is problematic because the pertinent personal information you previously gave your listing agent could be relayed to others in the firm. Consumer advocate Ralph Nader worked to stop this form of agency.

✓ **Transaction Brokers** or **Nonagency Agents** only represent themselves. Technically, they are not "agents" because they do not represent any party. In practice, a transaction broker works as a manager of the transaction, facilitating the sale but not favoring any party.

11
CHAPTER

Shady Agent Scams to Get Your Listing

Large Firms Are No Advantage

Unsure how homes are actually sold, many agents from large multi-office firms will sell you the benefits of listing with a big broker. The bigger is better idea may seem to make sense, especially if the firm has boatloads of For Sale signs in your neighborhood.

But the size or the perceptual dominance of the firm that lists your home is meaningless because you are not hiring the firm, you are hiring the agent. The 2005 study by Geoffrey K. Turnbull and Jonathan Dombrow for the National Center for Real Estate Research found "There is no evidence of pervasive performance advantages for larger firms...for either listing or selling functions."

Fear Tactics: List with Our Firm or Else

Agents may claim they only show their firm's listings. This is Shady Agent baloney. Agents do not control the market; buyers and sellers do. All buyers use the Internet sites like Realtor.com to find homes they want their agent to show them. Should an agent not show a home a buyer wants to see, the buyer will always find another agent who will.

The Invisible Buyer

While advertising your home as a FSBO, a Shady Agent will claim to have a buyer for your home and ask to "preview" it. Once inside, the agent will invariably find an excuse as to why the home is not a "good fit" for his buyers and then pressure you to sign a listing contract.

The Imposter Buyer

While selling as a FSBO, a Shady Agent may call and ask to show your home to a buyer. What you do not know is that this so-called buyer is really another agent or friend pretending to be a buyer. After the showing, the Shady Agent will invent an excuse why the buyer did not like your house. The Shady Agent's modus operandi is to establish she has plenty of buyers and then make a pitch to list your home. If you list with this Shady Agent, you can expect more of the same nonsense.

Your Home Is Missing from MLS

Just as the listing contract with your current agent nears its expiration date, a Shady Agent seeking your listing will call and ask, "Is your home still for sale, because I cannot find it in MLS?" In reality, the home is properly listed in MLS but the Shady Agent wants you to doubt your agent's competence. If you list with this interloper, you can expect more of the same chicanery.

"We Sell All the XYZ Corporation's Transferees"

Corporate transferees are good buyers because they are gainfully employed and must buy quickly. Knowing that, Shady Agents will claim their firm has the "exclusive relocation contract" for all the employees at the XYZ Corporation when in fact no contract exists. They perpetrate the lie by inserting phrases into their advertising such as: "XYZ Corporation transferees are welcomed to view this magnificent center hall colonial…"

When the Listing Expires, They Suddenly Have a Buyer

When your listing contract expires, you will receive letters and calls from agents claiming to have a buyer for your home. These claims are usually false and used as a ruse to gain access to you and your home. Should you let one of these agents inside, he/she will invariably say your home is not a match for the hypothetical buyer but then begin pressuring you to sign his/her listing contract.

12
CHAPTER

How to Discount the Commission

Before the Internet, the MLS database was an intranet accessible only by member brokers. Agents used this inaccessibility to justify their six percent commissions claiming it was needed to advertise the property to potential buyers. The Internet eliminated the need for advertising and paying high commissions.

A discounted commission may be defined as paying less than what most agents charge. This usually means paying four percent or less a flat fee as low as $99. plus 2.5% to the buyers' agent. Agents can refuse to negotiate or lower their commission, but the law prohibits them from implying that the fee is set by custom or some authority like the Realtor trade group or a government agency.

Some brokers openly advertise their discount fees, but if you cannot find a discount broker, here's how you can negotiate a lower fee from a firm charging more. Soon after a prospective listing agent arrives at your home, ask what fee or commission the agent charges. An honest agent will immediately answer with a concise and definitive answer. Shady Agents will act surprised or insulted and respond with the following:

- ✓ The standard fee has always been 6 percent.

- ✓ I work too hard to charge less.

- ✓ The fee is used to promote your home.

- ✓ No one in this area discounts commissions.

- ✓ If you find an agent to list at a lower rate–it's a scam.

- ✓ Homes listed with discount brokers never sell.

- ✓ Buyer agents blacklist homes listed by discount brokers.

- ✓ No broker can provide the proper level of service at a discount.

- ✓ The fee is predicated on the complexity of the transaction.

- ✓ A higher commission will result in a higher sales price.

- ✓ You get what you pay for.

Some agents will ask how much you want to pay. Before you answer, know that nearly all agents will discount a 7 or 6 percent fee by 1 percent. When offered a discounted commission, be sure the commission quoted includes the fee paid to the buyers' agent. Some Shady Agents will quote a low fee and then wait until you are signing their listing contract before explaining you must also pay an additional fee to the buyers' agent. Shady Agents have a habit of "forgetting" important things.

Other Shady Agents will put you off, claiming they need to check with the broker/owner before reducing the commission. Most will come back and explain they can discount if you promise to buy a home through them. Dismiss these agents; they do not want to help you.

How to Reduce the Commission

Most firms do not openly admit they discount commissions. However, many quietly permit their agents to discount the firm's portion of the commission by 1 percent. Secondly, they always allow agents to cut their portion by 1 percent or more. Hence, if the firm will not reduce the commission the agent usually will.

Some agents will offer to discount if you also agree to buy a home through their brokerage. Avoid such entanglements. Should an agent not lower the fee to your satisfaction, ask another agent in the same office or call another firm.

CHAPTER 12

<u>Discount Brokers</u>

If you think agents charging 7, 6, or 5 percent are overpaid for the service they render, list with a discount broker. Many discounters offer the same services as conventional brokers charging more.

If you cannot find a discounter, know that many single-office firms quietly operate a discount service within their full-service brokerage. All you have to do is ask for a discount.

<u>Menu-Based Discounters</u>

Some discounters will list your home in MLS for a low flat fee and then let you select and pay for additional services you think are necessary. You can save tons of dough if you know what you are doing. Unfortunately, some of these discounters prey on inexperienced do-it-yourselfers by using bait-and-switch tactics. They never clearly explain that you will need these additional services until you have signed the listing agreement and paid their low upfront fee. Here are some examples of their additional services and corresponding fees:

- ✓ Installing a "for sale" sign - $75.

- ✓ Installing a lockbox - $125.

- ✓ Printing color brochures - $50.

- ✓ Holding an open house - $250.

- ✓ Negotiating the sales contract - $500–$1,000.

- ✓ Attending the home inspection - $250.

- ✓ Posting photos on Realtor.com - $450.

- ✓ Meeting with municipal inspectors - $300.

<u>Internet-Based Limited-Service Discounters</u>

Internet-based discounters have websites instead of offices and can be found by searching the Internet using keywords like "discount MLS" or "flat-fee real estate." These websites charge $250 to $1,000 to list your home in MLS. Be warned, many of these discounters merely refer you to a local do-nothing agent who uploads your home to MLS and disappears. Should you ever need an experienced agent to solve or negotiate a problem, there's no help coming.

For Sale by Owner (FSBO) Websites Offer MLS Too

To compete with conventional brokers, most "For Sale by Owner" websites offer to upload your home to the local MLS for about $750. They merely refer you to a local broker who uploads your home to MLS and is never seen or heard from again.

The Buyer Broker Commission Scam

Posted on your home's MLS data sheet is the amount of commission you are offering buyer brokers to deliver a buyer for your home. When paying a total commission of say 5 percent, you should pay at least one half (1/2) of that commission to the buyers' agent. Hence, your listing agent will keep 2.5 percent and the MLS data sheet will denote buyer brokers will be paid 2.5 percent. Check the MLS datasheet to be sure you haven't been tricked into paying your listing agent more than what you are offering buyer agents.

Shady Agents have been known to reduce the buyer agent's share of the commission listed on the MLS datasheet without their sellers' knowledge and pocket the difference at closing. This scam is easy to pull off because few sellers ever review the MLS data sheet prepared by their agent and therefore never confirm the commission offered to buyer agents. To prevent this dishonesty, many states require the amount offered to buyer agents noted on the listing contract.

13
CHAPTER

The Tricks and Traps of the Listing Contract

Before you meet with prospective listing agents, ask them to bring all the documents you will need to sign if you decide to list. Take a day to read the documents without the agent standing over you and pushing a pen in your hand.

<u>Listing Contracts Protect the Agent</u>

Shady Agents prefer to call listing contracts "listing agreements" because it sounds less threatening. Be warned, nearly all listing contracts are written for the benefit of the agent and read something like this:

"In consideration of the Listing Broker listing and endeavoring to find buyers or tenants for the property at the listing price, the owner grants the listing broker the exclusive right to sell, lease, exchange, or otherwise transfer property, at the listing price and on the terms as stated in this agreement or upon such other price and/or terms that may be acceptable to the owner.

The listing broker is directed by the owner to list the property with the MLS and distribute this listing to other member brokers..."

Other than listing your property in the MLS database, most listing contracts contain nothing about what the agent will while the property is listed in MLS. There is no mention of preparing a market analysis, attending inspections, qualifying buyers, installing lockboxes and lawn signs, taking photos, measuring rooms, advertising, posting to Realtor.com, negotiating, posting directional signs, delivering contracts, follow-up on showings or holding open houses.

The bulk of the document is legal verbiage explaining how much commission you will pay and when. Agents defend these one-sided listing contracts by claiming the services are implied, i.e., "trust us."

List the Agent's Responsibilities on the Listing Contract

Once you sign the listing contract, most agents follow the simplistic selling plan outlined in Chapter 4. They upload your property to MLS, install a lawn sign and lockbox, make a brochure, and then wait for a buyers' agent to deliver an offer. When that doesn't happen, they simply wait for you to run out of time and then suggest you lower your asking price. That is just about all they do—but you can do better.

Your agent should provide a written list of what he or she is responsible for. A listing agent's responsibilities include, but are not limited to, the following:

1. Prepare and deliver a competitive market analysis of property.
2. Measure all rooms for the MLS data sheet and property brochure.
3. Take all photographs for MLS and Realtor.com.
4. Research and confirm property zoning on MLS data sheet.
5. Immediately upload property with photos to MLS.
6. Review copy of uploaded MLS data sheet with owner.
7. Install lockbox.
8. Install lawn sign.
9. Install box for property brochure on lawn sign.
10. Add rider or insert for lawn sign if needed.
11. Return all phone calls from owner.
12. Prepare and print property brochure.
13. Showcase property with at least 15 photographs on Realtor.com.
14. Prepare the property disclosure form with sellers.
15. Promptly make any changes to MLS data sheet that seller deems necessary.
16. Handle all buyer broker inquiries concerning the property.
17. Follow up on all agent previews—get feedback.
18. Follow up on agent showings—get feedback.
19. Follow up with buyer agents on any possible offer.
20. Financially qualify agent's or buyer agents' buyers.
21. Handle all contract negotiations.
22. Present all offers in a timely manner.
23. Evaluate and consult with sellers about contract of sale.

CHAPTER 13

24. Confirm contract and documents have been delivered to all parties.
25. Coordinate and attend all inspections.
26. Verify that mortgage application has been made.
27. Verify that earnest monies have been deposited.
28. Verify that appraisal has been completed.
29. Handle home inspection issues with buyers' agent.
30. Handle issues with any changes in scheduled closing date.
31. Verify whether buyers' lender requires new survey.
32. Verify buyers' loan will be ready to close on time.
33. Schedule fire inspections as required by law.
34. Attend smoke and carbon-monoxide inspections.
35. Attend final inspection with the buyers and/or buyers' agent.
36. Secure keys and garage door remotes for closing.

Optional clauses could be more specific:

✓ Agent will hold open houses on the following dates: 1/6, 1/13, 1/20, 1/27.

✓ Agent will run ad in the local paper every weekend for the duration of the listing.

Do not list with an agent that refuses to put promises in writing. If the agent claims the MLS does not permit additions to the MLS agreement, find another agent.

The Breakable Listing Contract—Your Malicious Agent Removal Tool

It is easier to find an agent than it is to get rid of one. Thankfully, the law requires that all listing contracts have an expiration date. Shady Agents will imply a six-month or one-year contract is the "standard listing period." This is baloney. There is no "standard listing period." Never sign a listing agreement that is longer than ninety days unless it is breakable with some sort of kick-out clause, such as:

"The seller may terminate this listing contract with a three-day notice. The property will be withdrawn from MLS, and the owner will be released from the contract and owe nothing to the listing broker."

Shady Agents argue against breakable listing contracts by claiming they need a minimum amount of time to justify their "investment" in listing the property. This is more Shady Agent baloney. When an agent will not guarantee service by offering a breakable contract, the agent is serving notice you may not be satisfied. The majority of real estate agents do not offer breakable listing agreements because they need to keep your property tied up long enough for another broker to deliver a buyer so they can get paid.

Retain the Right to Sell It Yourself

Adding the following clause to your listing contract gives you the right to pay only the listing portion of the commission when you find your own buyer:

"When the seller procures his/her own purchaser, the sellers will pay only the listing portion of the commission (2.5 percent), and the listing agent will assist the sellers through the duration of the transaction."

With this clause, your agent is still getting paid for the work he or she did: uploading the home to MLS, taking photos, installing the yard sign and lockbox, and helping you determine the asking price. The chances you will find your own buyer are slim, but not impossible.

14
CHAPTER

Pocket Listing Scams

There are two kinds of pocket listings: one that happens without your knowledge and the other you foolishly agree to. Both occur when Shady Agents purposely fail to upload your property to the MLS database with the aim of selling it themselves and collecting the entire commission.

<u>The Pocket Listing Scam You Foolishly Agree To</u>

A Shady Agent may offer you a discounted commission provided you permit the agent to "exclusively" market your home for the first 30 days of the listing contract. This means for the first 30 days of the contract, other agents will not know your home is for sale. The agent will claim he can sell your property without MLS because he and his firm have plenty of their own buyers. The agent will claim his "exclusive" listing arrangement will prevent countless "looky-loos" from traipsing through your home. He goes on to say you have nothing to lose because if he does not find a buyer within thirty days, the home will be uploaded into MLS for all buyers and brokers to see.

In reality, the chances the agent will find a buyer without MLS are slim. The Shady Agent's ulterior motive is twofold. First, he/she wants to eliminate other agents from competing for your listing by baiting you with a low commission. In thirty days the listing will then morph into an unbreakable "sole and exclusive right to sell" at a higher commission rate of 5 or 6 percent. Second, he/she may have a secret buyer as described in the next section.

When Your Agent Has a Secret Buyer

The second type of pocket listing is more insidious than the first because it happens without your knowledge. After signing the listing contract, you expect your agent to immediately upload your home to MLS—but he doesn't because he already has a buyer for it. Just after signing the listing contract, the agent will call and say something like, "I just found buyers looking for a property exactly like yours but we have to act fast as they are leaving town tomorrow."

Your agent then shows the buyers your home, prepares a contract, and pressures you to sign it by saying: "I know the price is not exactly what you want, but your first offer is always your best and if you pass on this buyer, your home will be sitting on the market for months. If you sign now, you can get on with your life."

Under tremendous pressure, you ask for $10,000 more. Shameless, the agent immediately calls his buyer with the speakerphone on so everyone can hear. You can cut the tension in the room with a knife. The agent tells the buyers they can have the house if they agree to pay an additional $10,000. The buyer pauses and says he will "meet halfway" and pay $5,000 more. The agent stares at you for a response and then pushes a pen at you to sign the contract. With no time to think, you nervously nod yes." The agent gives you a wink and triumphantly says, "I hope you're happy; I just got you $5,000 more!" Your home is sold, and as your agent drive away, he calls the buyer to congratulate him on "stealing" your house.

Back at the office, the Shady Agent now uploads your house to the MLS database and marks it "sold." He does this to gain credit toward his top-agent sales award. But your home was never available to other members of MLS and their buyers. Perhaps you would have received full price or even multiple offers—you will never know.

How to Prevent the Pocket Listing Scam

After signing the listing contract:

✓ Confirm your home has been uploaded to MLS by immediately requesting a copy of your MLS data sheet.

✓ Be certain the MLS denotes the home as "active" or "available."

✓ If a lockbox is employed for showings, be certain it is installed immediately, *especially if your agent or your agent's firm is already showing your home to buyers.*

CHAPTER 14

✓ Be sure your listing agent and his firm are telling buyer agents your home is available to show. The MLS database may show the listing as available, but your agent may be telling other agents the home is no longer available, has contracts pending, is sold, or is temporarily off the market.

✓ Be certain the agent has not posted comments that restrict showings on the MLS data sheet such as: "All appointments to show through listing agent."

✓ Listings uploaded to Realtor.com appear within hours, so check to be sure your home is there. If not, it is probably not in the MLS database.

Avoid any agreement that does not include uploading your home to MLS. No firm has more buyers than the local MLS. Without MLS, you are paying an agent to bring a buyer who does not have to compete for your home on the open marketplace. Should you sell without MLS, you will probably receive less.

15
CHAPTER

How Your Home Appears in MLS: The Data Sheet

Nearly all of the information your agent uploads to the local MLS about your home is then automatically uploaded to Realtor.com—the Internet site most buyers use. Your listing agent is responsible for how your home is presented in MLS and subsequently on Realtor.com.

Within 24 hours of signing the listing contract, get a copy of your home's MLS data sheet. Check it to be sure your agent has uploaded all pertinent information. Check Realtor.com to be sure the agent has uploaded at least 15 photos. Be warned that incompetent agents may use outdated information about your home obtained from an old listing and/or have the office receptionist prepare and upload the listing.

Listing data sheets with factual errors have legal consequences for sellers when buyers hire a lawyer who claims the information provided was a "wanton and reckless misrepresentation of the facts used to induce the sale."

Getting a copy of the MLS data sheet also confirms your agent has not made your home a pocket listing (see Chapter 14, "Pocket Listing Scams").

Common Input Mistakes Made on MLS Data Sheets

Most of the time, mistakes and omissions made by your agent on the MLS data sheet will only hinder the sale of your home. Here is what to look for:

- ✓ *Wrong property type* - The agent may have submitted your home to the condominium, co-op, or multifamily section instead of single-family homes, where it belongs. Buyer agents will never find it.

- ✓ *Wrong geographical section or town* - Your agent uploads your home to the wrong town, where it remains unseen by agents in your area.

- ✓ *Confusing showing instructions* - Showing your home must be easy. (See Chapter 23, "Make It Easy for Agents to Show Your Home.")

- ✓ *Directions to the home are incorrect or missing* - Read the directions your agent has written very carefully. Dismiss any agent that simply instructs agents to use their GPS.

- ✓ *Incorrect phone numbers* - Be sure buyer agents can make an appointment.

- ✓ *Understated property taxes* - At closing the buyer may demand damages for the additional tax to be paid while he owns the property.

- ✓ *Incorrect lot size* - This happens when agents rely on an old source or make it up!

- ✓ *Missing or incorrect room sizes or square footage* – when overstated buyers could eventually sue claiming a misrepresentation of a material fact.

- ✓ *Empty fields* – incomplete data sheets reflect on the property.

- ✓ *Failure to mention extras that build value* – amenities such as skylights, Brazilian cherry flooring, and radiant or multiple zone heat; brand-name appliances such as Sub-Zero®, Bosch®, Thermador®, or Viking®; and finishing materials such as marble and granite.

- ✓ *Meaningless remarks* – "charming", "cozy", "a must see", "hurry won't last", "close to Star Bucks".

- ✓ *Agent's text description degrades home's value* - "This home is a diamond in the rough, needs TLC," or "Owner will credit buyers $5,000 toward new carpet and paint," or "Wet basement has been waterproofed."

- ✓ *Failure to highlight special value* – items like possible subdivision or commercial use.

CHAPTER 15

✓ *Incorrect zoning* - if the buyers' eventual use of the property is deemed illegal, the buyer will no doubt find a lawyer and sue. For example, writing "large garage perfect for in-home business or landscape operation" implies that the property is legally approved for commercial use.

Personal Property: Included or Excluded

Things permanently attached to walls, ceiling, or floors are legally known as appurtenances and considered part of the property: dishwashers, ovens, ranges, ceiling fans, light fixtures, built-in bookshelves, fireplace doors, window treatments, and under-cabinet lighting.

A microwave sitting on a countertop is not an appurtenance, but if your MLS data sheet denotes a microwave, buyers can rightfully assume it is included with the home. The same holds true for the refrigerator, the backyard jungle gym, storage sheds, gazebos, portable hot tubs, fireplace tools, and pool accessories.

Items you do not want included with the sale must be specifically excluded in writing before the contract of sale is finalized. Be careful when listing an item as "excluded" on the MLS data sheet. It may bring attention to the item, encouraging buyers to include it with their offer. To prevent this, keep all personal property off the MLS data sheet—whether included or excluded. When an offer is received, you and your agent should check if any personal items have been added to the contract. When including personal property with the sale, insert a clause into the contract specifying the item is sold in "as is" and with no warranty.

Photographs

Your home's listing must have *at least* 15 - 25 good-quality photographs. Agents and buyers assume listings with just a couple of photos have a problem. Taking and submitting photographs is your agent's responsibility. Since photos of your home are uploaded to Realtor.com, visit that site to check their quality. Some agents have a talent for taking great photos and enhancing them with software like Photoshop or Paint Shop Pro. Taking quality photos using a point and shoot camera with a built-in flash is nearly impossible. For best results, your agent should hire a professional photographer who takes advantage of existing light using a wide-angle lens and a remote flash.

✓ Replace or correct crooked photos.

✓ Remove clutter before photos are taken.

✓ Never get cute and include pets or people in the photos.

✓ Remove cars and boats from the driveway.

✓ Close garage doors and remove garbage cans from view.

16

CHAPTER

How Your Home Appears on Realtor.com

There is no reason not to have your home on www.realtor.com. A day after signing the agent's listing contract, search Realtor.com to confirm your home is on the site. If you cannot find it, then buyers cannot find it and your agent may not have submitted it to MLS. Know that nearly all multiple listing services upload their properties to Realtor.com. Hopefully your agent has not made your home a pocket listing (See Chapter 14, "Pocket Listing Scams.")

Homes on Realtor.com include most of the data your agent has uploaded to the MLS database except for personal information like your name and phone number. If the Realtor.com listing is missing information or photos, your agent has probably not entered them into the MLS database. It is imperative that you review both the local MLS data sheet and the Realtor.com web listing to be sure they are complete and have at least 15 good-quality photos.

Agents who pay an additional fee can "showcase" your home on Realtor.com. The "showcase" option allows your agent to post twenty-five photos and a 2,500-character description. It also includes bells and whistles like a video tour, two different headlines, and the posting of open-house dates. But it is more important that your agent has meticulously included all the information needed to build value in your property.

17
CHAPTER

Determining Your Home's Value—An Overview

Rule #1: Research the Value of Your Home

Rule #1: You must have a rock-solid understanding of your home's value before listing it in MLS. Not knowing its value will exacerbate problems throughout the selling process. Most sellers determine their home's market value by one or more of the following:

- ✓ Visiting websites Zillow or eappraisal.com.

- ✓ Rumor of what a neighbor's home sold for.

- ✓ Multiplying what they paid by some inflation or deflation factor.

- ✓ How much money they need.

- ✓ Wait to see what an offer brings.

Few sellers will pay an appraiser $350. to obtain an appraisal when they know a real estate agent will prepare a market analysis for free. Competitive market analyses (CMA) or a brokers price opinion (BPO) are better than nothing but they are not as reliable as an appraisal. The problem is most CMAs and BPOs do not include or compare the square footage of similar homes. Instead, they merely list the number of rooms making it easy for the agent to manipulate the estimated value. Hence, sellers never have a good understanding of their home's value.

As the months roll past with few showings and no offers, sellers who fail to heed Rule #1 from Chapter 17, blame their agent for inadequate marketing and relist with another agent promising more promotion. The process repeats itself until the seller runs out of time and is forced to reduce the asking price (sometimes below market value).

To best way to determine the accurate market value of your home is to get an *opinion* from a real estate agent and the *facts* from a licensed appraiser.

Upgrades that Add Little or No Value

The value of any upgrade or feature in your home is its ability to convince someone to buy it. Individually, upgrades rarely increase a home's value beyond the item's actual cost. Here are some examples:

- ✓ Masonry fireplace vs. modular fireplace

- ✓ Bamboo floor vs. oak floor

- ✓ Forty-year roof shingles vs. thirty-year shingles

- ✓ Vinyl siding vs. wood shingles

- ✓ Upgraded lighting fixtures vs. builder grade

- ✓ Granite countertops vs. laminate

- ✓ Composite Trex® deck vs. wood deck

- ✓ Gas cooking range vs. electric

- ✓ Granite tile vs. ceramic tile

- ✓ Sheetrock basement ceiling vs. suspended ceiling

- ✓ 42″ kitchen cabinets vs. standard 32″ cabinets

- ✓ Wood floors vs. wall-to-wall carpeting

- ✓ Professionally sodded lawn vs. seeded

- ✓ Brick or stone front vs. clapboard/vinyl

- ✓ Custom window treatments vs. store-bought curtains

CHAPTER 17

- ✓ Brand-new carpet vs. old carpet

- ✓ Brand-new HVAC vs. older model

- ✓ Bay or bow windows vs. double hung

- ✓ Corner lot

- ✓ Decks & patios

- ✓ Back-up generators

- ✓ In-ground pool

- ✓ Spa or hot tub.

Features That Always Increase Value

- ✓ A well-known, highfalutin neighborhood.

- ✓ A school district with a top ranking.

The Value of Pools

Whether a pool adds value to a property depends on whether pools are a common feature of nearby comparable properties. By the same token, not having a pool in an area where they are prevalent may deflate value. Above ground pools add little or no value because they are considered personal property. Generally speaking, pools only have value if desired by the buyer. The photo shows what became of a pool when a home owner tired of paying for the chlorine and electric to run the filter.

18
CHAPTER

Using an Agent to Price Your Home

Agents are eager to provide a free comparative market analysis (CMA) or a broker's price opinion (BPO) because it gives them the opportunity to convince you to list with them. Dismiss any agent who charges a fee to prepare a CMA or BPO and/or claims it to be equivalent to an appraisal. A CMA or BPO is *not* an appraisal. Only licensed appraisers can legally prepare an appraisal and be paid for it.

Real estate agents arrive at a home's value by *subjectively* comparing comparable properties based on location, curb appeal, condition, and school system. They rely on their experiences with buyers and arrive at a value based on what they think a buyer will pay.

A common problem with agent CMAs is their use of comparables matching the style and room count of the subject property while ignoring the square footage of each home. It is extremely important that sellers review the CMA carefully. Make an effort to drive by the comparable properties used in the agent's report.

<u>Buying the Listing</u>

Shady Agents will try to decipher what you think your home is worth before preparing their market analysis or offering their opinion. They may be blunt and ask, "What are you looking to get?" They may be devious: "Do you think your neighbors got enough money for their home?"

Once an agent knows what you want, he/she will begin hinting that it may be worth more. This tactic is called "buying the listing." If you fall for the ruse and list with the agent, the agent will return a few weeks later with a new comparable and argue the original asking price is too high. This is another reason why agents use unbreakable listing contracts.

Buying the Listing Up to the Next Higher Price Level

Shady Agents take the tactic of "buying the listing" to another level when they convince sellers to increase their home's asking price above market value. They claim the higher price will deliver more buyers because, "…recent statistics show buyers are looking for homes in the next higher price level." Greedy sellers fall for this logical fallacy because it seems plausible.

For example, when your home's market value is $390,000, the Shady Agent will say, "The last three houses sold in this neighborhood were priced about $450,000. So raising your price to that level will attract those buyers." When you take the bait and list with the Shady Agent, the agent knows it's only a matter of time before you reduce the price to its true value.

The Range Game

Shady Agents will beat around the bush and give a range of value, say $800,000–$875,000. If you get greedy and sign the agent's listing contract, inevitably the agent will begin nagging you to reduce it.

The Right Price and the Fear of Overpricing

Shady Agents have no intention of helping you get top dollar for your home. Their goal is to get it sold before the listing contract expires. They convince you to set the price below market value by conceding their recommended price may seem low, but then give a reassuring smile and say it's "the right price". Others will warn of the "dangers of overpricing":

- ✓ Your home will be listed too long and buyers will think something is wrong with it.

- ✓ Overpriced homes only help sell other homes.

- ✓ If it sells, the property will not appraise and the buyer will not obtain the loan.

The Buyers' Triangle

An agent may explain how to set price by drawing a triangle with parallel lines on a piece of paper. The top of the triangle represents the highest possible price for your home and the bottom is the lowest. In each section or price break, there will be a given number of potential buyers represented by dots.

The diagram assumes the lower the price of your home, the greater the number of potential buyers. The agent will warn that if you list it at the highest price, you will be forced to wait a long time for that one prospect to arrive. The agent is probably right.

19
CHAPTER

Using an Appraiser to Price Your Home

Relying solely on an agent to determine the value of your home is risky, especially when the agent wants your signature on an unbreakable listing contract. Get a second, objective opinion from a disinterested third party—a licensed appraiser. Be sure not to use an appraiser recommended by an agent you may use to list your home.

Appraisers Are Supposed to Be Objective

Unlike real estate agents, appraisers determine market value by objectively comparing comparable sold properties in the same or similar neighborhood. An appraiser's evaluation primarily considers the property's location, square footage, age, condition, and lot size. The value of amenities such as patios, pools, hot tubs, decks, garages and fireplaces are extracted from the marketplace, i.e., they are not assigned a cost or retail value. That means your pool costing you $56,000 may only be given a value of $10,000.

Nevertheless, appraisers are human and may be swayed by the condition of a home, so have yours appraised after you have prepped it for market.

Appraisal Cost and Use

Sellers of single-family homes may obtain what is known as a "restricted-use appraisal report" for about $350. The money spent will help you avoid questioning whether the agent's market analysis and your own best guess about your home's value are accurate.

Do not show the appraisal to prospective listing agents and do not include the appraisal with any promotional materials given to prospective buyers. Giving agents a copy before negotiations begin gives them time to find fault with it. Agents criticize appraisals by claiming they don't reflect where the market is heading. Let the parties know you are using the appraisal as a guide to obtain fair market value.

Finally, know that the value your lender's appraiser gave your home when you applied for a home-equity loan is unreliable. Appraisers are not paid much for home-equity appraisals so they merely make them "fit" the needed loan. Though banking regulations forbid lenders from revealing the loan amount to appraisers, appraisers routinely ask homeowners how much they are borrowing. So much for banking regulations to eliminate undue influence!

20
CHAPTER

How to Set Your Asking Price

Once you have obtained a CMA or BPO from an agent *and* an appraisal from a licensed appraiser, compare them but give more credence to the appraisal when determining market value.

<u>Avoid the Second-Guessing of Underpricing</u>

If you're greedy, go ahead and list your home price higher than the agent's BPO or its appraised value. But when a month passes with no activity, the market has spoken. Immediately reduce the price recommended by the BPO and/or appraisal. Statistically, sellers receive 96 percent of their last asking price.

<u>When Price Is Not an Issue</u>

Buyers and agents assume that homes unsold more than twelve months are either overpriced or have some other problem. They also know these sellers eventually run out of time and are susceptible to low ball offers. If your home has been listed at market value for months without an offer, you have likely overlooked a problem not related to its price. See Chapter 26, "Why Your Home Does Not Sell".

Hope Springs Eternal for the Buyer Willing to Overpay

Sellers who set their asking price above market value with the hope of finding a buyer willing to overpay usually wait a long time for that fool to appear. Nevertheless, here are buyers known to overpay:

- ✓ Relocated employees—especially from foreign countries.

- ✓ Buyers outbid on another home.

- ✓ Emotionally deranged by a new love or loss.

If you fancy yourself a riverboat gambler, go ahead and pay a 7 percent or 6 percent commission to an agent promising that superior merchandising will deliver a big spending buyer. Maybe you'll get lucky. But even if a buyer takes the bait and the lender's appraiser somehow makes the home's value fit the contract price, the lender's underwriter will probably reject the report and deny the loan, forcing you to reduce the contract price or find another buyer. Prudent home sellers set their asking price at or near its fair market value and avoid the hassle.

Price Breakdown—The End Game

Before setting your asking price above its fair market value, know the effort required to keep your home clean and ready to show is a woeful endeavor that will leave you susceptible to *price breakdown*. Price breakdown occurs when you run out of time and energy and must settle for a below-market offer.

Desperate sellers facing price breakdown are easy to spot in MLS. Their property's MLS data sheets have a high "days on market" number (DOM). Their agents have added comments like: "motivated sellers" or "please present all offers" or "owner will consider any reasonable offer." Note that most these comments appear without the sellers' knowledge.

Here is how price breakdown can happen: a couple impulsively buys a new home under construction that will be ready in six months. They then call an agent to sell their home, and the agent's CMA shows the home to have a market value of $500,000. But, needing money to buy the new home, they list it higher at $550,000.

Three months pass, but they receive no offers. Instead of reducing the price to market value, they stay the course. When the listing expires, they relist with a new agent promising more advertising and open houses but nothing happens. Out of time, the sellers obtain a bridge loan to close on their new home. They move all their furnishings out of their old home, leaving it vacant, and smelling of mildew.

A month later, they accept a $480,000 offer, but the home inspection reveals a cracked roof rafter. The crack is inconsequential, but another thirty days pass before all parties can agree on a resolution forcing the sellers to dump the home for $470,000. They also pay $6,750 to the builder in per-diem late fees and another $1,700 in interest for the bridge loan. Did I mention they also paid a 6 percent commission to their agent of $28,200? Yikes!

(SELLING PHASE)

21
CHAPTER

Offering Incentives to Sell Your Home—A False Hope

I have never found any empirical evidence proving that offering a financial bonus or incentive to agents or buyers will result in more showings or induce a sale. In fact, buyers have always questioned my motives for showing them a listing that promised to pay me a bonus over and above the stated commission. Secondly, I have never known a buyer to purchase a home just to collect a new flat-screen TV or new carpet. Besides, most agents have learned that bonuses are only paid if the home is sold at full price.

But hope springs eternal for frustrated sellers who learn of a sold home where the sellers offered an incentive and hastily conclude the freebie was responsible for making the sale even though there is no data proving such schemes work. In reality, the sale was made in spite of the incentive and the receiving party only collected the loot as part of the bargain.

Offering an incentive encourages low-ball offers because it conveys a message of desperation. The incentive may generate interest in your property, but enticing a low-ball offer and then somehow negotiating the offer up to market price is a long shot. Low ballers only bid on property to buy it below its fair market value.

Agents often convince sellers to offer and pay for a home warranty plan for prospective buyers. Unfortunately, these agents never tell the sellers they are receiving a kickback from the warranty company. The kickback is illegal, but it happens all the time.

The only sensible incentive is offering to pay a fixed amount of the buyers' closing costs. Since most buyers in this category use the low 3.5-percent-down financing through the FHA, it follows that these buyers would need cash to close. Note that FHA regulations require that the cash paid to the buyers at closing cannot exceed 6 percent of the purchase price. But there is no need to quibble over amounts; offering $5,000 may be all the buyer needs.

22
CHAPTER

The Value of Open Houses

Public Open Houses

Agents vying for your listing may promise to hold open houses, but they know the chances that anyone who shows up will actually buy the house are slim. The 2010 NAR Profile of Home Buyers and Sellers showed only 11 percent of buyers first learned of the house they purchased from an open house or a yard sign. This is why experienced agents persuade new agents to sit the open houses at their listings.

Many who attend open houses are looky-loos in search of decorating ideas or nosey neighbors who introduce themselves and say, "I've always wanted to see the inside of this house." A few may come to use the toilet. Nevertheless, if you want open houses, be certain you write that obligation on your agent's listing contract.

One good outcome of open houses is the objective criticism voiced by those who attend. Since they have no connection to you or your agent, they will eagerly offer comments about your

decorating, pet odors, floor plan, and all the other reasons why they don't like it. Hopefully your agent relays these comments to you.

Some agents generate traffic to open houses by sending invitations to homes in the surrounding neighborhood. Your home then becomes a quasi-branch office for the agent who will use a sign-in sheet to gather the contact information of neighbors who may be considering selling their homes. Know that Shady Agents routinely add fictitious names to the sign-in sheet with the aim of impressing their sellers with all the buyers the open house generated.

Broker Open Houses

So-called "broker" open houses are usually held during the work week with the intent of introducing new listings to buyer agents. To ensure a large attendance, they are scheduled the same day local real estate offices hold their weekly meeting. After the meeting, agents caravan to the open houses to enjoy the free coffee and cake used to entice them to attend. As the agents leave your home, the last agent's job is to shake your hand and with a wink and a smile say, "Don't worry, we'll sell it."

The "Lower Your Price" Raffle Scam

Your listing agent may use a broker open house as an opportunity to ask all the agents who show up to write their opinion of your asking price on the back of their business card. The cards are then deposited into a bowl for the chance of winning a gift. When the open house ends, your agent then shows you the cards with the price opinions on the back. Don't expect many cards to indicate your home is underpriced.

Open House Thieves

Some agents will claim open houses attract thieves. The chance your home will be robbed is extremely rare, but it has happened. You should remove valuable items you usually leave out, including bank and credit card statements. Doing this will not only prevent theft, but it will also prevent you from mistakenly believing something has been stolen when you have only misplaced it.

The Open House Launch or Sneak Preview Scam

Your listing agent may present you with a plan for an open house that resembles a product launch or sneak preview. The agent will claim that by listing your home in the MLS database and delaying showings until a future date will create excitement and pent-up demand. This is accomplished by inserting the following remarks on the MLS data sheet or For Sale sign: "No showings until Open House."

Be careful, Shady Agents use this tactic for the purpose of uploading your home to MLS so it appears on Realtor.com where he/she will receive buyer inquiries while competing agents are barred from showing and selling the home. The arrangement is another form of the pocket listing and may deny your chances of receiving the highest and best offer.

23

CHAPTER

Make It Easy for Agents to Show Your Home

Installing a lockbox on your front door is the easiest way for agents to show your home to buyers. Your agent's MLS may employ an electronic lockbox system that records when the box was opened and the name of the agent that opened it. Although the box can be programmed to operate only between 9:00 a.m. and 9:00 p.m., you should remember that selling your home requires sacrifices, and sleeping after 9 a.m. on weekends is one of them.

Make Showing Instructions Simple

The specific instructions on how agents are to show your home are determined by you and posted to your home's MLS datasheet by your listing agent. When using a lockbox, the buyer agent is usually instructed to call you to schedule the showing. If you are not at home, the agent will leave a message explaining when the home will be showed. If you are not home when the agent arrives, the agent will open the lockbox that holds the key to your home. Review your MLS datasheet carefully because complicated instructions deter showings:

✓ *Listing agent must accompany all showings.*

✓ *Twenty-four-hour notice required before showing.*

✓ *All appointments must be made twenty-four hours in advance.*

✓ *Key must be picked up at listing agent's office.*

✓ *Appointment required—dogs!*

If you have not instructed your listing agent to add such directives, then your agent is incompetent or may be purposely discouraging showings so she can sell it herself and collect the entire commission. You will never know for sure unless you review a copy of the MLS data sheet.

Some sellers expect their listing agent to be present at all showings. This restricts showings, but some agents are happy to act as a security guard to justify a hefty commission. But you can avoid the fear of theft by simply removing valuables from view or from the house altogether.

Requiring your listing agent to schedule the showing appointments of other agents may be problematic because if your listing agent is unreachable, the showing may be lost. Instructions that dictate the key to your home must be picked up at your listing agent's office are old-fashioned and will hinder showings.

Be Ready to Show at a Moment's Notice

Never refuse a showing because you think your home is a mess. The agent and buyers will usually move on to the next home and possibly be gone for good. Most agents will gladly give you time to straighten the home up; just don't take all day.

24
CHAPTER

Why Shady Agents Secretly Disable House Keys

When buyers tell their agent, "We want to make an offer on this house," the agent will immediately fear losing the sale to a competing offer. So as the buyers are leaving the house and no one is looking, the Shady Agent will disable the house key by rubbing its teeth against a brick step. The agent will then return the damaged key to the lockbox.

When another agent attempts to show the property, the key will not open the lock. By the time this agent contacts the listing agent to ask why the key does work, the Shady Agent (who ruined the key) has already delivered an offer to the sellers. Oblivious to the shenanigans of the Shady Agent, the listing agent tells the buyer agent not to bother with an offer because the home has already been sold—by the Shady Agent.

There are many ways to obtain the same results, like locking a deadbolt from the inside and leaving the house from a self-locking patio door. No matter how the trick is played, the seller never receives the benefit of a second offer and perhaps selling at the home's full market value.

25

CHAPTER

Keep Your Mouth Shut

While scheduling an appointment to show a home, a seller asked me if my buyers wanted a "real contemporary." When I asked why he explained his home had plain white walls, trapezoid windows, metal railings, and cathedral ceilings. He admitted he was having trouble selling because buyers found his home "too contemporary." Our chat convinced me not to show the house to my buyers. The home is probably still for sale!

Sellers should avoid conversations with buyer agents and their buyers. Your listing agent is responsible for all communications. Sellers usually contradict something their agent told the buyers or their agent. Secondly, the buyers may not believe what the sellers tell them.

Shady Agents Seek Personal Information

It is unethical for buyer agents to discuss anything with sellers whose homes are listed with another broker. But that will not stop them from pumping them for pertinent information. When agents and buyers come to see your home, shut up and get out of the house. Never hang around and say, "If you have any questions, just ask me." Let the buyers and their agent get needed information from your listing agent because that's his/her job.

A common trick used by Shady Agents is to claim your listing agent is "unreachable." This is a lie used to trick loquacious sellers into inadvertently revealing their bottom-line price or motivation for selling. The agent will ask an innocuous question like, "Did you get the permits for the garage?" The query is designed to ensnare you in a conversation wherein the agent will inevitably ask, "Have you had any offers?" How you respond will affect any ensuing negotiations. Direct that agent to contact your listing agent.

Dismiss your listing agent if he/she directs buyer agents or their buyers to call or text you with questions about your home. All communication between you and the buyers' agent is really negotiating, and all negotiations must be handled by your listing agent.

Keep Dad Away from Buyers

The most garrulous sellers are men, because they view their home as their castle and enjoy giving guided tours. Unfortunately, the king of the castle always talks too much when he explains:

- ✓ "The stain on the kitchen ceiling was from a clogged toilet."

- ✓ "The galvanized pipes in this home leak from time to time."

- ✓ "This carpet is a good carpet. We've had it over twenty years."

- ✓ "The lawn tractor is included in the sale, as are all the appliances."

- ✓ "Don't worry about the asbestos insulation in the basement."

- ✓ "We need to sell because we bought another house."

- ✓ "We received an offer, but it was too low."

- ✓ "We lost a sale because of home-inspection issues."

- ✓ "We are in no hurry to move."

- ✓ "We are downsizing because I was laid off."

- ✓ "The neighbors have barking dogs."

- ✓ "The school taxes are high but the schools are very good."

Using a lockbox gives you the opportunity to get out of the house before the buyers arrive, eliminating any chance of saying something stupid to the buyers or their agent.

26
CHAPTER

Why Your Home Does Not Sell

When six months pass with few showings and no offers sellers should reevaluate their selling strategy and more importantly, their asking price. Sellers with homes on the market 12 months or more are ignoring a problem.

You and your agent should have discussed anything that would hinder the sale of your home before listing it in MLS. Before you waste more time relisting with another agent, (promising to aggressively merchandise the property) take an objective second look at common problems affecting the marketability of all homes.

Price

Your home may be overpriced. Go to Chapter 17 and see Rule #1.

Showing Accessibility

Review the showing instructions on your MLS data sheet to be sure they are not too restrictive. For best results always use a lockbox and read Chapter 23, "Make It Easy for Agents to Show Your Home."

Location, Location, Location

- ✓ Busy road.

- ✓ School system with problems.

- ✓ High-crime neighborhood.

- ✓ Nearby high-voltage power lines.

- ✓ Odors from farm or sewer treatment facility.

- ✓ Designated wetlands or flood zone.

- ✓ Neighborhood with a pejorative nickname, e.g., Mechanicsville, Shantytown

- ✓ Home positioned below street level.

- ✓ Property taxes higher than adjacent towns.

- ✓ Barking dogs in neighboring yard.

- ✓ Nearby nonresidential use properties, e.g., school, parking lot, church, store, water or cell tower, airport, railroad, or cemetery.

Curb Appeal

Look at photos of comparable homes on Realtor.com to see how your home's cosmetic condition compares. Buyers do not want to redecorate a home unless they receive a discount from the asking price.

Architectural and Functional Obsolescence

Homes renovated without an architect by do-it-yourselfers usually have rambling layouts disliked by most buyers, e.g., eliminating a dining room to enlarge the kitchen, eliminating closets to enlarge a bedroom, replacing a garage with a family room, or installing an indoor pool or spa in a poorly ventilated space. Older, museum-like homes maintained in near-perfect condition may be fun and interesting to look at, but few consider buying them because their kitchens and baths remain outdated.

Unresolved Defects

Persistent water problems, aluminum wiring, high radon levels, polybutylene plumbing, asbestos, underground storage tanks, synthetic stucco, and structural or title problems must be remedied before listing your home in MLS. Buyer agents are quick to broadcast problems of a listed home to other agents.

CHAPTER 26

Once your home is repaired, do not broadcast the repairs made on the MLS data sheet. Comments like "new septic installed" or "oil tank replaced with EPA approval," or "water issue resolved" create a bad impression. Including repaired items on your property disclosure form is enough.

Stigmatized Property

Homes where a well-publicized event like a homicide or suicide occurred usually have no option but to transform the home through renovation, reduce the price below market value, or patiently wait for an unconcerned buyer.

Low Zillow Zestimate

Sellers have problems justifying their asking price when an automated value website like Zillow.com or eappraisal.com posts their homes value lower than the price listed in MLS. Agents and their buyers use those sites to condemn a seller's asking price.

Zillow claims their posted values (known as Zestimates) are calculated using a proprietary formula based on public and user submitted data. Knowing that, Zestimates should only be used for entertainment purposes because they are based on the computer science principle known as GIGO or garbage in, garbage out.

27
CHAPTER

Why Some Buyers Disappear

Keeping your home clean and available for showings is a full-time job. Your exasperation is compounded when seemingly interested buyers disappear and never heard from again. Fearing something is wrong with your home, you ask your agent for some feedback. Many times the feedback given are false objections because the buyers have issues unrelated to your home:

✓ Young buyers wrongly expected a parent to provide the down payment.

✓ The buyers concluded a new home will not save their marriage.

✓ Soon after leaving your home the buyers bought a new car and no longer qualify for a home loan. Never underestimate that new-car smell!

✓ The buyers are looky-loos not really interested in buying a home, but their nitwit agent shows them houses anyway. Tomorrow they will consider buying a boat or a timeshare in Tahiti.

✓ A buyer expects a salary increase that never materializes.

✓ Buyers have only five years left on their current mortgage and decide they do not want another 30 year loan.

✓ Your listing agent told the buyers' you prefer not close until after the holidays, but the buyers cannot wait that long.

✓ The wife wanted to impress her friends with a new house, and the husband went along with the charade until time came to sign the offer.

✓ The buyers learn they will not get enough money from the sale of their home.

✓ The buyers' home has not yet sold.

✓ The buyers were engaged to be married, but when the time came to make the offer, the fiancé decided he could not afford the bride.

✓ Using feng shui as a guideline, the buyers believe your house is facing the wrong direction.

(NEGOTIATING PHASE)

28
CHAPTER

Negotiating Offers

Rule #1: Know Your Home's Value

Don't even think of negotiating an offer until you are absolutely certain of its market value (see Rule #1 Chapter 17). Without knowing that number, you will be at the mercy of your agent who may throw you under the bus to secure the sale at a lower price.

If you have obtained a written appraisal as suggested in Chapter 18, you will have evidence agents will find hard to counter—though some will try. With an appraisal in hand, you can legitimately argue you are only seeking fair market value.

Negotiating Defined

Negotiating is a process to get from point A to point B. Never negotiate with the aim of beating the other party. Negotiating is not an "us versus them" event. Do not concern yourself with the great deal the other party is getting. Do what's good for you.

Your Negotiating Strategy and the Rules of Engagement

Your listing agent must handle all negotiating and have enough information about the buyers to formulate a strategy before responding to an offer. Always consider the buyers' reaction to your counteroffer. Here are some rules for you and your listing agent:

- ✓ Your listing agent will handle all communications You will not communicate with the buyers or the buyers' agent

- ✓ Your listing agent will verify the buyers are financially qualified

- ✓ You will be informed of all verbal offers; i.e., offers not in writing

- ✓ No response will be given to verbal offers until put in writing

- ✓ You will obtain a copy of any offer you respond to

- ✓ Your agent will be present if the buyers' agent presents the offer in person

- ✓ You will not divulge any other offers you are currently negotiating

Initial Talk of Offer May Contain Exaggerations and Lies

When there is talk of a potential offer, much posturing and misinformation may be offered by the buyers' agent. Problems will arise if you and your agent fail to separate truth from fiction. Here are some common lies made by agents:

- ✓ Your home is overpriced and will not appraise

- ✓ Your home needs too much repair work

- ✓ The buyers already have a mortgage commitment

- ✓ The buyers do not need a loan because they are paying cash

- ✓ The buyers will close in thirty days

- ✓ The buyers don't care about the condition of the house

- ✓ The buyers will not perform a home inspection

- ✓ The buyers' home has already sold

Once the offer is presented in writing, earlier verbal promises may disappear, especially if both agents are now working together to close the deal. Is it any wonder they call them Shady Agents?

Negotiate Price First

The ultimate sales price of your home is paramount. Do not get distracted with the other terms of the offer such as the closing date, the type of loan, and the personal property included in the sale. Negotiate price first and revisit those details later.

The Lazy Agent Contract Shuttle

Lazy agents negotiate by shuttling the offer back and forth between parties with the hope of eventually meeting in the middle. When the buyer raises the offer $5,000, the listing agent expects the seller to lower his/hers by the same amount, and so on. Agents who play this game like to boast they negotiate using a "win-win" strategy. They like to say, "Let's split the difference." In reality, the agents are working together to ensure the deal gets done and they get paid. To avoid the contract shuttle, you and your agent should discuss a strategy before negotiations begin.

The "I Need to Meet with You Now" Tactic

You know you will be receiving a disappointing offer if an agent insists on meeting with you before revealing the offered price. The get-together is used by the agent to pressure you to sign. The only negotiating strategy the agent has is to get paid. If possible, have the agent e-mail you a copy of the offer before meeting. Even if the offer is ridiculously low, you may not want to dismiss it completely.

Information Is Power

Negotiating success is attained by knowing all you can about the buyers:

- ✓ What is the buyers' current housing status?

- ✓ Are the buyers financially qualified?

- ✓ What are the buyers' incomes?

- ✓ What kind of jobs do the buyers have and where do they work?

- ✓ What kind of home do the buyers have now?

- ✓ Have the buyers recently tried to buy another house?

- ✓ How much cash are the buyers putting down?

Your Listing Agent Must Help the Buyers' Agent When Needed

Incompetent buyer agents with little negotiating experience need all the help your agent can give them. Be sure your listing agent doesn't discourage offers by making bombastic comments to buyer agents like, "Don't waste my time, your time, and my client's time with a low offer." Antagonistic ultimatums are deal killers serving no positive purpose.

Do Not Get Greedy and Blow It

Coercing buyers to pay more than fair market value is risky business unless the market is booming or your agent has information about the buyers justifying such action. Even when successful, bumping buyers may result in a case of buyers' remorse. The affliction begins shortly after signing the contract when they realize their irrational exuberance has caused them to pay more than market value causing them to cancel the contract.

Offers from Investors

Investors search MLS for desperate sellers willing to sell their home below market value. The only viable reason to sell your home to an investor is to prevent a disaster like foreclosure. Selling to investors is tricky because their business model requires sellers to lose so they may win.

Verbal Offers

As a rule of thumb, responding to a verbal offer is problematic because they are used to decipher your bottom-line price. Inform the buyers that you will respond if the offer is put in writing.

On the other hand, inexperienced and incompetent buyer agents sometimes present verbal offers because they do not know how or they are too lazy to write a valid offer. No, I'm not kidding. Before you send the buyers' agent packing, your agent should be sure the offer has no merit.

Prequalification Letter Must Accompany Offer

A lender's prequalification letter must accompany any offer because the majority of agents are incapable of financially qualifying buyers themselves. As explained in Chapter 32, "The Near-Worthless Prequalification Letter," these letters do not guarantee a buyer will obtain a loan, but an offer presented without one should be deemed suspicious.

The Faux Cash Buyer

Knowing many are awestruck by big money, agents will use the false promise of having a cash buyer as a means to discount the price of your home. To support the scam, the written offer will not include a loan contingency giving the impression the buyers are paying cash. Amazingly, your agent may too fall for the ruse and never ask the buyers' agent for proof the cash exists. Foolishly impressed, you discount the price of your home.

However, once the contract is signed the buyer may try to insert the loan contingency into the contract with a claim like, "For tax purposes my accountant feels I should get a loan". Other times the buyer takes his chances and applies for the loan without the contract having a loan contingency. You'll discover the ruse when the lender sends an appraiser to your home. By then it's too late and you've been had. You have no alternative but to hope the buyer obtains the loan and closes on the property.

Dealing with Agents During Negotiations

Always let your agent handle negotiations. Do not talk with the buyers' agent and never meet with or talk to buyers. The only reason the buyers' agent would want to talk with you is to learn your bottom-line price or gain a concession. Never allow a buyers' agent to present an offer to you without your listing agent present.

When the buyers' agent and your listing agent work for the same firm, they have probably discussed the offer and formulated a strategy before meeting with you. The agents may claim they haven't, but that's baloney. Not only do agents from the same firm work together to make the sale, but the office manager or the firm's broker will see to it the negotiations end successfully—for *them*. (See Chapter 30, "What Agents Say behind Your Back—Everything!")

Negotiating Pressure Tactics

You know you are about to be coerced to sign a bad contract when the agent:

- ✓ Avoids phone contact and insists on meeting with you.

- ✓ Discusses everything about the contract but the sales price.

- ✓ Pushes a pen at you.

- ✓ Involves the broker or office manager in the negotiations.

- ✓ Asks how much you owe on the property.

- ✓ Asks for your bottom line price.

- ✓ Claims your home will not appraise for asking price.

When Your Listing Agent Has an Offer

Pity the sellers who believe their listing agent has their best interest at heart when that agent is receiving both the selling and listing portions of the commission. Agents refer to such a sale as "a home run." Doubling the commission doubles the agent's motivation to push the deal forward, regardless of your best interests.

Never Reveal Your Bottom-Line Price—Shut Up!

When an offer is imminent, speak to no one but your listing agent and avoid hypothetical pricing discussions with your agent and buyer agents who will try to engage you in a conversation with the aim of learning your bottom-line price.

How to Handle Pushy Agents

When a Shady Agent begins coercing you to accept a low offer, let the agent know you would be willing to reduce your price if the commission is reduced proportionally. The comment usually quiets him/her.

When the Buyers Need to Sell Their Home—The Right of First Refusal

When you agree to an offer that includes a contingency giving the buyers the right to sell their home before closing on yours, be sure your home remains listed in MLS and available to other buyers until the buyers' home has sold.

Be extremely wary of buyers who claim they plan to sell their home to a friend or relative, as these sales are rarely consummated. Do not sign a contract of sale before verifying their home is already listed in MLS. Your contract could include something like this "right of first refusal" clause:

> This contract is contingent upon the buyers selling their home, which is currently listed in the local multiple listing service. The seller shall keep his home listed in the MLS and should the seller receive another offer, the buyer has the right to match this offer and immediately proceed to closing. In the event the buyer does not match the new offer, this contact shall become null and void, and all deposit money will be returned to the buyers.

The Danger of Creating False Competition

When negotiating, avoid playing games like pretending to have another interested buyer. It will discourage buyer agents, who will not waste their time trying to sell a home they assume is already sold. More importantly, should they discover that no other buyer exists, your credibility will be lost forever.

How Shady Agents Block Multiple Offers

When negotiating an offer delivered by your listing agent or your agent's firm, be sure your agent is not telling other agents your home is under contract or sold. This tactic eliminates competing offers and prevents you from obtaining the highest possible price. Another tactic is to change the status of your home in MLS from "active" to "under contract" or "pending" when negotiations begin. If you suspect your agent is playing games, check Realtor.com to be sure the home is still available for other offers.

<u>Buyers' Remorse</u>

Once the contracts are signed and legally binding, do not immediately permit your agent to mark your home as "sold" and remove it from the MLS database. In rare instances the buyers' initial euphoria becomes remorse, causing them to cancel the contract. Your agent should not report the property sold until the buyers have applied for their mortgage and paid their loan application fee. You will know that that has happened when the lender's appraiser arrives at your home.

29
CHAPTER

How Not to Handle Low-Ball Offers

<u>Macho Bernie</u>

I prepared an offer for first-time buyers on a tired ranch listed at $299,900. When I arrived at the house to present the offer, the seller's agent introduced me to the seller who was a older and frail widower. We all exchanged niceties and then sat down at the kitchen table, where I passed out copies of my buyers' offer.

Just then, a short, pudgy man in his late sixties came out of a bathroom just off the kitchen. He was stuffing his shirt into his unzipped pants while he held a folded newspaper tucked under one arm. The man made his way toward me and loudly said, "OK, what have you got?" Not knowing who this guy was, I looked to the seller's agent for help. She told me he was a friend of the seller and his name was Bernie. The seller said nothing.

I acknowledged Bernie and opened my folder showing my offer of $350,000. Bernie dropped his newspaper on the table and reached over and picked up the offer with one hand while still holding his pants and belt buckle in the other. He looked at it for a second, and then flung it at me like a Frisbee and blurted, "How dare you insult us with this crap. Take it and get out!"

The ladies didn't know what to do. The listing agent looked down at her papers on the table, and the widowed homeowner got up and left the room. There was dead silence.

I tried to think of something to say to this jackass, but I just picked up my offer and left.

I convinced my buyers to find another home.

Bernie did what he did to impress his widowed girlfriend. I don't know if Bernie ever got his woman, but I do know the buyers would have increased their initial offer if they had gotten the chance.

Always Counter a Low-Ball Offer

When confronted with a low-ball offer, remain calm and businesslike. Do not become emotional and make enemies with the buyers or their agent. Acting angry and indignant may cause you to lose credibility with the agent, who will relay everything you say to the buyers. Never assume the low-ball offer is all the buyers are willing to pay—even if the buyers' agent argues it is. The buyers may have ulterior motives for making the low offer their agent knows nothing about.

Never counter a low offer with a bombastic "No" unless you can risk permanently ending negotiations. Most sellers do this to exact revenge because it makes them feel good. A better course of action is to act like an adult and counter the offer with the idea of moving the buyers' offer up. Negotiating is a process to get from point A to point B. Counter the offer or ask the buyers' agent to resubmit the bid and convey the message that you are interested in selling but the offer is just too low to counter.

At best, you will have a day or two to respond before the buyers grow impatient and move on. Most negotiating lasts only a couple of days. Rarely does it last more than a week. However, there are rare instances where buyers quit negotiating but return weeks later to make another offer.

Why Buyers Make Ridiculous Low-Ball Offers

✓ Fear: many low bidders are first-time homebuyers who are scared silly about buying a home. These buyers usually increase their offer.

✓ Posturing: well-intentioned, serious buyers will low ball in an effort to lower the sellers' expectations. Their initial low offer conveys the message they will not pay top dollar for the property.

✓ Priming the pump: the agent suggested the low price as a means to convince nervous buyers to sign the offer. These buyers will usually increase their offer.

✓ Probing: to determine how firm you are on the price by your response.

✓ Looky-Loos: they are searching for that imaginary seller who will give his home away. These buyers are a waste of time.

✓ Investors: they make low-ball offers because their aim is to make money when they buy a property; i.e., they buy below market value.

30 CHAPTER

What Agents Say behind Your Back—Everything!

Licensing law requires agents to protect and promote the best interests of consumers. But when a sale is imminent, most agents assume the role of middlemen and work together to ensure the deal gets done and they get paid. A typical conversation between agents goes something like this:

Buyers' agent: "Hello Suzy, I showed your listing today. It's been on the market awhile; can you tell me if there's anything wrong with it before I write up an offer?" Translation: Tell me what price the seller will accept.

Listing agent: "Well, the owners recently reduced the price and are very anxious to sell." Translation: They'll give it away.

Buyers' Agent: "That's what we thought. We didn't see any men's clothes in the closets, so we assume the sellers are divorced. Did the husband move out?"

Listing agent: "He's gone, and he lost his job. I don't know how he can afford the house, his new apartment, and his girlfriend!"

Buyers' Agent: "That's too bad. The kitchen needs updating but my buyers want to offer $850,000. What do you think?"

Listing agent: "The kitchen is a disaster, and the baths need to be redone too. They already turned down an offer of $850,000, but if offered again, I think they'll take it."

Buyers' agent: "I'll see what I can do."

Listing agent: "E-mail me the offer, and we'll get it done."

When negotiating, always communicate with your agent verbally because agents routinely forward their clients' texts and e-mails to other parties.

31

CHAPTER

The Near-Worthless Prequalification Letter

Though license law requires agents to ascertain the financial qualifications of every person for whom he or she submits an offer, a majority of agents cannot mathematically qualify a buyer for a home loan. Hence, they fake it and rely on loan officers to qualify their buyers and provide what is known as a "prequalification letter." Lenders freely generate prequalification letters for agents, hoping they will steer borrowers their way. Agents then use the letters as indisputable proof their buyers qualify for the loan.

Do not be fooled by prequalification letters that "guarantee" the buyers will obtain the needed loan, because the borrowers' credit and employment history will not be verified until the borrower submits a formal loan application and pays the application fee.

The Nonexistent Mortgage Commitment

A Shady Agent may claim her buyers do not need a prequalification letter because they already have a "mortgage commitment." Do not accept this claim without inspecting a copy of the so-called commitment. It's common for agents to confuse a prequalification letter with that of a loan commitment.

Unlike a prequalification letter, a mortgage commitment reads like a contract because that's exactly what it is. It requires the signatures of both the lender and the borrower. Unlike a prequalification letter, it will enumerate the sales price, the length of the loan, the interest rate, the monthly payment amount, the expiration date of the commitment, and include the HUD good-faith estimate (GFA).

How to Know If Buyers Have Applied For Their Loan

Most contracts specify the buyers must immediately apply for a loan. You will know if the buyers have applied for that loan when their lender's appraiser calls to inspect and appraise your home. Appraisers only begin their work after the buyers have completed the loan application and paid the application fee. If no appraiser has called to inspect your sold home, it usually means the buyers have not yet applied for the loan.

Should the buyers' loan application process begin late, the closing will probably be delayed. Your listing agent is responsible for following up on the buyers' loan-commitment process.

3 2
CHAPTER

The Rent with Option to Buy Scam

A rent or option to buy contract gives a buyer the right or option to buy a property on a specified date. Before that date, the buyer rents the property, and that rental payment defrays the owners' expenses. If all goes as planned, the tenant will eventually exercise the option and close on the home. The option concept appears simple but due to the unsavory and unqualified buyers the scheme attracts, it often becomes a convoluted con game.

Here is how it goes down: a Shady Agent will seek a desperate seller (the mark) with an unsold property (a vacant home is a favorite target). Working with a buyer (the shill) who cannot immediately qualify for a loan, the Shady Agent will propose that the buyer rent the home and when ready, exercise the option and pay full price for the property. The Shady Agent convinces the buyer to pay full price to bait the anxious seller into accepting the deal (the con).

The Shady Agent will claim the "option to buy" is necessary because the buyer needs time to clean up his credit file and to save money for the down payment. The Shady Agent will also claim the buyer has little or no cash due to one or more of the following:

- ✓ A divorce

- ✓ Medical bills

- ✓ The death of a family member

- ✓ A foreclosure

- ✓ A job loss.

But none of the above is the true cause of the buyer's financial problems. Buyers seeking a rent-to-buy contract are grifters with little income and a bad credit history. They are incapable of upholding any kind of contractual agreements—be it a contract of sale, a credit card, or a marriage. They are lifetime renters who conspire with Shady Agents looking to make a fast buck.

Rent to buy or option contracts are doomed from the start because they cannot possibly provide for all the unknown events that will occur while the unreliable and credit less buyers occupy the property purportedly saving for their down payment.

<u>How It Gets Ugly</u>

A few months after signing the rent to buy contract and moving in, the so-called buyers stop paying rent and claim a leaking pipe has damaged the floor and ceiling creating an "unsafe living condition that denies the quiet enjoyment of the premises". But the pipe is not broken. Instead, the buyers have allowed water from the shower curtain to leak onto the floor ruining the ceiling below. When the owner investigates, it becomes clear the tenant has invented the problem as a reason not to pay the rent. The parties begin fighting, and the seller sues for eviction.

The buyers' lawyer countersues, claiming they cannot be evicted because the option contract gives them an "equitable interest" in the property. Over the next year or so, an expensive legal battle ensues while the tenants live in the home rent-free. Eventually the sellers agree to a settlement wherein they return a good portion of the rent received and the buyers move out.

When the sellers regain possession of their home, they find it trashed. Worse, they must relist the property in MLS and search for another buyer.

<u>How Investors Make Money Using the Option to Buy</u>

Unscrupulous investors with no intention of selling their property trap gullible subprime buyers into option to buy agreements. The investor uses the scam as a means to collect the rental payments until one day (as expected) the buyers are late paying the rent. The investor then evicts them, pockets their down payment, and begins searching for another victim.

(UNDER-CONTRACT PHASE)

33
CHAPTER

Your Agent's Responsibilities after the Contract Is Signed

When you have signed a contract of sale, your adventure with the buyers has just begun. Be warned that as soon as contracts are signed, most listing agents will hastily install a "sold" sign and remove your home from MLS, believing their job is done. However, your listing agent has a responsibility to ensure the sale successfully closes on time.

The key word here is "time." Your agent must pay attention to contract contingency dates involving the inspections, loan application, appraisal, and the loan commitment. Time does not favor a seller who has removed his home from the market (MLS). While you're busy making moving plans, unknown problems may arise and threaten the scheduled closing.

Your Agent's Responsibilities

- ✓ Provide you with a readable copy of the contract

- ✓ Provide you with the entire original contract and all addendums

✓ Confirm all parties have a copy of the contract and any addendums

✓ Confirm all contract changes have been initialed by all parties

✓ Confirm the closing date on a periodic basis

✓ Provide you with a copy of the buyers' loan qualification letter

✓ Provide written confirmation that the escrow money has been deposited

✓ Confirm the location of the deposit money

✓ Confirm your home is not yet marked "pending" or "under contract" in MLS

✓ Confirm the buyers have made their loan application

✓ Confirm the appraiser has completed the appraisal

✓ Confirm the sale of the buyers' property if required to purchase yours

✓ Confirm all the home inspections been scheduled

✓ Attend all inspections

✓ Deliver a copy of the inspectors' reports within three days of the inspection

✓ Confirm all inspections are complete

✓ Confirm the closing date—again

✓ Resolve inspection issues; agent does *not* let them hang

✓ If inspection issues not resolved, confirm your home remains listed in MLS

✓ Confirm all contract contingencies have been satisfied

✓ Update the progress of the buyers' mortgage commitment

✓ Confirm the closing date—again

✓ Confirm all municipal permits required to close will be obtained.

CHAPTER 33

When to Report Your Home "Sold" to MLS

When your listing agent changes the status of your home in MLS from "active" to "pending" or "under contract," the home will no longer be available to any other potential buyers. Be warned, listing agents who sell their own listing are quick to remove the home from MLS to protect it from another competing offer.

Do not allow your agent to report your home as sold until you are certain the buyers have not caught an acute case of buyers' remorse (see next section) and are considering breaching the contract. Secondly, talk with your agent about the possibility of the buyers not successfully completing any of the contract contingencies. If you think your agent has reported your home sold too soon and without your permission, search for it on Realtor.com. If it is not there, it has been removed from the MLS database.

How to Handle Buyers' Remorse

Just after signing a contract, buyers may become conflicted about the purchase and develop what is commonly known as "buyers' remorse." You know this is happening when after signing the contract, the buyers ask to revisit your home to:

- ✓ Show it to another family member

- ✓ Measure for window treatments

- ✓ Confirm a piece of furniture will fit.

Whatever the reason, do not let the buyers back in your home until the scheduled inspections. Buyers who want to revisit a home immediately after buying may be looking to find a reason to change their minds. To gain access buyers may circumvent their agent and contact you directly. Do not talk to them. This is not the time to become friends with them or their agent. Your agent's is responsible for all communication with the buyers and their agent.

Most buyers become committed to the purchase after they have paid the home inspector and loan application fees. Buyers who have a valid reason to change their minds will do so during the home inspection. Hopefully your agent will be ready for any surprises.

The "Missing Deposit Money" Scam

It is the fiduciary responsibility of your listing agent to confirm the buyers have paid the deposit or escrow money as specified in the contract. Incompetent agents commonly forget to follow up on the whereabouts of this money.

Sometimes, buyers have enough money to cover the deposit, but they do not immediately have the cash on hand and need more time to withdraw the funds from some sort of investment account. A Shady Agent may disguise this problem by happily providing a copy of the buyers' deposit check, but that check is never deposited. Your agent must confirm the disposition of the escrow funds in writing.

Should the buyers decide to break the contract, you may expect to keep their deposit money only to find it was never collected! Should you then sue for that money, you will be tied up in a protracted and costly legal battle. Most sellers in this situation have no alternative than to release the buyers from the contract and relist the home in MLS.

34
CHAPTER

The Dreaded Home Inspector

Home inspections became of age during the growth of consumerism in the 1970s. Today the inspection is mainly used as a tool to renegotiate the contract sales price. There are three types of home inspectors:

- ✓ Those who minimize problems, insuring the sale closes and the agents get paid;

- ✓ Those who exaggerate defects so the buyers can renegotiate the contract price;

- ✓ Those who honestly complete the inspection.

To curb unethical relationships between agents and inspectors, many states prohibit inspectors from compensating agents for sending them customers. Nevertheless, agents routinely recommend "friendly" home inspectors to their buyers.

Examples of Creative Writing by Home Inspectors

In return for sending them customers, inspectors will tweak their reports as suggested by buyers' agents who prep inspectors with comments like, "My buyers are concerned about the cracks on the front steps and the old furnace." The inspector will then write: "Masonry porch has dangerous cracks and should be replaced" and "Furnace has outlived its useful life and should be replaced." Here are other examples:

- ✓ Hot water heater is functional, but due to its age should be replaced.

- ✓ Roof is approaching its life expectancy and should be replaced.

- ✓ Recommend removal of overhanging trees.

- ✓ Recommend replacement of cloudy Thermopane windows.

- ✓ Recommend replacement of rusty electrical panel box.

- ✓ Structural engineer needed to determine integrity of sagging floor.

Though most homes do not have serious defects, most inspectors will find something to justify their inspection fee of $350–$800. Secondly, the reports are written to assume the worst to protect the inspector from being sued by the buyers if something fails after the buyers move in.

Minor Problems Inspectors Routinely Mention in Their Reports

- ✓ Loose bricks or mortar; e.g., driveway retaining wall, steps, and chimney

- ✓ Loose railings

- ✓ Loose ceramic tile

- ✓ Water stain on ceiling

- ✓ Low water pressure

- ✓ Although not leaking—older roof

- ✓ Rust on circuit-breaker box

- ✓ Loose ground wire in circuit-breaker box

- ✓ Nonexistent ground fault interrupter plugs (GFI)

✓ Rust spots on metal fireplace box

✓ Rotting wood on porch, deck, or trim

✓ Stove burners not working properly

✓ Missing caulk around windows and doors

✓ Evidence of active termites

✓ Evidence of past termite damage

✓ Poorly vented attic, basement, or crawl space

✓ Yard with inadequate drainage

✓ Cloudy Thermopane windows

✓ Skylight with evidence of past leakage

✓ Black mold anywhere.

Where Sellers Should Be During the Inspection

Sellers should not attend home inspections because their presence serves no positive purpose. When sellers are present, the buyers or the inspector will bring them into a discussion about a suspected problem. Unfortunately, when defending their home, sellers are usually perceived as liars.

Your Agent Must Attend the Inspection

It is your listing agent's responsibility to be present at all inspections. Some realty firms quietly tell their agents not to be present to avoid being dragged into any litigation brought on by buyers who close on the property and subsequently find a defect.

Your listing agent may say something like, "It is unlawful for me to be present with the buyers and their inspector because it is a conflict of interest." This is Shady Agent baloney. Your listing agent must attend the inspection to learn if any found problems are of concern.

Your Agent Must Know Construction

Agents who know nothing about construction or the operation of systems such as the HVAC, plumbing, and electrical are nearly useless as real estate agents.

Clean Well-Kept Homes Make Inspectors Lazy

Like buyers, home inspectors assume a clean home has also been well maintained and therefore problem-free. Since they are not expecting trouble, they do not look for any. This is especially true of newer homes.

Late Reports Are Always Trouble

Negotiating away defects found by an inspector become problematic when the inspection is performed late and/or the report is delivered beyond the time period (usually ten to fourteen days) set forth in the contract. This happens when your listing agent is not paying attention to the contract contingency time periods. Sellers are at risk when their listing agent installs a "sold" sign and proceeds to do nothing but wait for the closing to be paid. While weeks pass without other prospective purchasers, the current buyers will have the upper hand renegotiating the contract sales price using the defects in the inspection report as bargaining chips.

You can claim the inspection or the report was late and hence, null and void. But contract inspection dates are difficult to enforce unless the phrase "time of the essence" is in the contract. Nevertheless, it is your listing agent's job to be sure the buyers are performing as specified in the contract of sale.

How to Get a Leg Up on Late Reports

While waiting for the results of the buyers' home inspection, be sure your home remains listed in MLS. This will cause the buyers' agent to worry about losing the sale to another buyer insuring the inspections are performed in a timely manner. Do not flaunt this tactic and be careful not to distress the buyers. Although no law requires homes under contract to be removed from MLS, you need to maintain a respectful relationship with the buyers. Should they complain that the home remaining listed in MLS shows you are not acting in good faith, delist the home because you've made your point.

How to Negotiate Defects

When the buyers' inspection report is delivered to the seller, it may come with a specific list of defects the buyers want corrected. Other times, the report is delivered with the implication that everything in the report should be corrected or the buyer will not complete the purchase. Do not panic and read on.

The overwhelming majority of home inspections do not reveal major defects. Most find minor problems, which are used to renegotiate the contract price. Your listing agent is responsible for handling these negotiations. This is why your agent should attend the inspection and learn which defects really concern the buyers and those being used to renegotiate the contract sales price. Be warned, many buyers' agents and listing agents will conspire to determine what each party will settle for because they want the sale to close so they can get paid (See Chapter 30, "What Agents Say behind Your Back.")

Most inspection reports include items like broken door locks, bad electrical outlets and circuit breakers, water stains, and loose ceramic tile. Respond by taking the high road. Proudly agree to repair issues that affect the buyers' safety, i.e., electrical wiring, smoke or carbon monoxide detectors, loose handrails and steps, bad water quality, high radon levels, or lead paint. Doing the right thing will give you credibility to explain away other problems.

How to Barter Away Defects

When your agent prepared your multiple listing data sheet, hopefully he/she did not include any personal property with the home sale. Items such as window treatments, refrigerators, washers, dryers, lawn equipment, and pool furniture can be used to barter away the petty repairs the buyers demand. Instead of replacing a window with a broken Thermopane seal, give the buyers your lawn tractor or your window treatments.

Another way to prevent haggling over a home inspection report is to lower the buyers' expectations by adding the following clause to the sales contract: "The home is sold as is, and the seller will not pay more than $100 for any repair(s)." The clause may not stop buyers from trying to negotiate, but it lowers their expectations.

There's No Negotiation on Large Defects

Negotiating away a major defect like a failing foundation, a cracked sewer line, a bad septic system, aluminum wiring, or extensive termite damage is extremely difficult. Most buyers will not complete the purchase unless you make the repair.

You may argue that your house was sold "as is," but you risk the buyer cancelling the contract. You can then threaten to sue for specific performance, but no court will direct a buyer to purchase a home with a major defect. If you cancel the contract and find another buyer, know that you and your agent will be legally obligated to disclose the defect to any new buyer.

Avoid DYI Repairs

Avoid repairing a defect found by the home inspection yourself because buyers are rarely satisfied with the workmanship. Instead, offer the buyers a personal item like the extra refrigerator in the garage, the window treatments, the lawn tractor, or the snow blower. If you have nothing the buyer wants, obtain an estimate for the repair from a licensed contractor and offer to credit the buyer the cost of the repair at closing.

Defects No One Knows How to Handle

Home inspectors can create a world of problems when they recommend a "specialized professional" is needed to evaluate some enigmatic defect. The buyers or their agent will naturally exaggerate the mysterious problem and threaten to cancel the transaction.

If not dealt with promptly, the problem will take on a life of its own. The aim of the ensuing drama is to obtain a large monetary concession from you, the seller. Your listing agent should have the know-how to quickly determine exactly what the problem is and how to solve it before the buyers gain control of the transaction. This is usually accomplished by bringing in your own licensed architect or structural engineer who presents a simple remedy.

Defects Not Requiring Repair

The inspection report may list items that are not compliant with current building codes. A common complaint is the lack of ground fault interrupter (GFI) plugs in the kitchen and baths. If GFIs were not required when your home was built, you may have no legal obligation to elevate your home to current construction codes. Your agent should confirm this with the local building inspector. Then again, you can buy a GFI plug for about nine dollars, install it yourself, and be done with it.

How to Lower the Expense of a Significant Defect

When the home inspection reveals a defect in a major system costing thousands of dollars, it is often assumed the seller is obligated to provide full replacement or full credit to the buyers for its cost. This is not always true. Buyers may agree to split the cost based on the fact they will be getting a new system.

Condos and Co-ops

Defects found in exterior items such as roofs or decks in condominiums or Co-ops are usually covered by the association or Co-op board. Exceptions may include items known to quickly wear out or break: windows, exterior doors, heating and air conditioning units, plumbing, etc. Who is responsible for what is found in the association or Co-op bylaws. Usually you can placate the buyer at a closing by writing a letter to the association and demanding the defect be corrected. A few buyers will assume the association will do the work and close on the unit even if the repairs have not been made.

Inspectors Doubling as Contractors

Any inspector that includes repair estimates with his report and/or offers to make repairs or recommends a contractor must be considered a scoundrel. You can reject the report and report the inspector to the American Society of Home Inspectors (ASHI).

35
CHAPTER

Termite Inspections

All lenders require a certificate from a licensed pest exterminator showing the home to be free from wood-boring insects such as termites, powder post beetles, carpenter ants, and carpenter bees. If the inspector finds infestation, the insects must be exterminated and proof of extermination must be presented to the lender before closing.

Sometimes the buyers' home inspector will perform the wood-boring insect inspection. Other times the home inspector will employ a friend in the pest control business. Be warned that an inspection performed by an extermination company is more likely to find infestations than a home inspector, because they are looking for the job to exterminate. The cost of extermination begins at about $500.

If no living insects are found, inspectors will search for the remains or body parts of dead insects and/or their excrement (frass) as proof of infestation. To avoid this, vacuum dead insects and their debris from your floor, windowsills, and sill plate before the inspector arrives. The sill plate is the horizontal piece of lumber on which the house sits atop the foundation.

If the inspector finds dead pests, you could clean up them up and then pay your own exterminator to perform an inspection. With no insect parts to be found, your exterminator may give you a certificate with a one year guarantee you can then forward to the buyers. Know that not finding insect parts doesn't necessarily mean your home doesn't have a wood boring insect problem.

36
CHAPTER

Septic Inspections and Buried Fuel Tanks

<u>Septic Systems</u>

If your home is not connected to a public sewer and utilizes its own septic system, expect buyers to have it inspected. Septic inspectors find problems with nearly all systems because buyers routinely sue them should the system fail after closing. An inspector in my area has the reputation of failing all the systems he inspects. Agents recommend him to buyers looking to gain a new system or price concession from the sellers.

Home inspectors that double as septic inspectors usually do a lousy job inspecting septic systems. Most merely flush dye down a toilet and then judge the system on whether they find that dye rising to the surface in the yard. Some will fail a system if they detect a septic odor in the yard—even when the odor is naturally coming from a plumbing vent pipe on the roof! When this type of cursory inspection fails a perfectly good system, you can aggressively question the competence of the inspector or find your own inspector to contradict the results. But winning that battle is a long shot—especially if your septic system is old.

Most competent inspectors perform what is known as an "open pit" inspection, where the lid is removed from the septic tank. Water is then loaded into the tank by turning on all the faucets in the house. If the level of fluid in the septic tank rises, it usually means the leach field cannot handle the discharge because it is clogged or damaged. Hence, the system is failed. Competent inspectors will insert a video camera into the leach field to support their conclusion.

Septic inspectors will suspect a problem already exists if they find signs of amateur repairs, e.g., laundry waste being diverted to a ditch or dry well. Chatty sellers who foolishly talk too much about their septic may cause the inspector to believe they are hiding a problem. To prevent this, sellers should not attend the inspection—it's their agent's job. Before the inspection begins, your agent should give the inspector copies of receipts proving you were diligent in cleaning the system every three years along with a copy of the system's construction plans.

If you already know a problem exists, get it repaired *before* you call an agent to list your home. Do not list your home for sale with the hope the problem will not be found or with a plan to credit the buyer for the cost of a new septic system. Buyers and their agents do not want to get involved with complicated projects and will find it easier to buy another home.

Have a copy of the original septic design on hand for the inspector. Knowing where the integral parts of your system are located will help the inspector and allay his suspicions.

If the system needs to be repaired or replaced, be certain you obtain the proper permits for the work because buyers will want to see them. Employing your neighbor with a backhoe to repair the system (at night) is problematic because the inspector may notice the repair and ask to see the permit. And should buyers close and then find your repairs were made illegally, their lawyer will seek damages for fraud.

When you have repaired or replaced a septic system, do not broadcast or advertise this fact on your MLS data sheet with phrases like "brand-new septic installed." The comment will only cause buyers to worry about the other major systems of your home. Allow buyers to discover the new septic as the transaction progresses.

When a septic fails inspection and a buyer demands a new one, there is usually no other alternative but to replace it because the inspector may be required by law to report the failed system to the local health department.

Buried Fuel Tanks

If your property has a buried fuel tank, remove it and replace it with a new aboveground tank *before* you meet with an agent to list the home in MLS. Do this work with appropriate government permits. No buyer will get involved with a property that includes a buried fuel tank because the cleanup responsibilities enforced by the government are outrageously expensive and never ending.

(CLOSING PHASE)

37
CHAPTER

The Closing-Day Stickup

While conduction their final inspection just prior to closing, my buyers noticed a couple of landscape lights were broken. At the closing the buyers demanded the sellers replace the busted lights because their home's MLS data sheet included the remarks: "professionally landscaped with low-voltage lighting." But the sellers refused and responded with a bombastic "take it or leave it." So my buyers got up and left. Shocked, the sellers' agent ran after my buyers and persuaded them to return to the closing table by promising to pay for the lights herself.

Buyers will use the stress of closing day to satisfy unresolved issues to their advantage. Your listing agent *must* attend the final inspection to handle and/or explain away any complaints buyers and their agents may look to find:

✓ Nail holes from picture hooks

✓ Household trash left behind

✓ Lawn not cut

✓ Woodpile or swing set left in yard

✓ Furniture left in house

✓ Paint cans in basement or garage

✓ Missing pool accessories

✓ Moving truck damage to lawn

✓ Dirty house

✓ Damage to walls or flooring

✓ Wet floor from leaking refrigerator water line

✓ Missing light fixtures and/or ceiling fans

✓ Missing fireplace doors and tools

✓ Missing window screens

✓ Missing lawn tractor included with sale

✓ Missing garage door remotes

✓ Stove burners not operating.

Municipal Inspections

Before closing, your town may require a "certificate of occupancy," which may include a smoke and carbon monoxide alarm inspection. Know that city hall and its inspectors are often uncooperative and unprofessional. They rarely schedule inspections at specific time. Instead, they schedule them sometime in the morning or sometime in the afternoon, expecting you to wait for them to show up. When paying a 7, 6 or 5 percent commission, be sure your listing agent is responsible for scheduling and attending all municipal inspections and obtaining required certificates.

38
CHAPTER

The Closing

The act of transferring title or ownership of your property to the buyers by signing a new deed and receiving payment occurs at the "settlement" or "closing." Closings may take place at the buyer agent's real estate office, the buyers' title company, or a lawyer's office. The real estate agents will attend to pick up their check.

Closings are a hectic time, and many are postponed and rescheduled. Most times the lender is behind schedule because of missing paperwork.

Hopefully your agent has obtained any required occupancy permits and/or smoke and carbon monoxide detector inspection certificates needed to close. Don't forget to get credit for items like fuel oil remaining in your tank or the prepaid balance remaining on your security system contract.

Review the HUD-1 Closing Statement Carefully

How the money from the closing is collected from the buyer and disbursed to the seller and associated parties is itemized on the HUD-1 or closing statement. The figures on the HUD-1 are derived through simple mathematics so mistakes happen. Review the statement carefully. It is nearly impossible to correct a mistake after a closing, so if you have a question about anything on the HUD-1, be sure to ask your attorney or the title agent to explain it.

SHADY AGENTS™

Check the Agents' Commission on the Closing Statement

Most sellers never review the agents' commission invoices because they are usually submitted directly to the title company that prepares the HUD-1 closing statement. The only chance a seller has to review the statement is usually during the closing. Mistakes are often overlooked because closings are a stressful event. Can you see the mistake in the following?

Commission due Shady Agent Realty:
Sales price $650,000.00 x .025 (2.5 percent) = **$17,500.00**.

The commission should only be $16,250. Also, check the agent's commission statement when the sales price of your home has been increased or decreased to compensate the buyers for repairs or closing fees. A Shady Agent will use the higher number to increase the commission. For example let assume the initial contract price was $650,000. To settle home-inspection issues, you agreed to reduce the sales price by $10,000. The commission should be paid on the $640,000 and *not* the original $650,000.

39
CHAPTER

When Buyers Refuse to Close

Keeping the Buyers' Deposit Money

In most instances, sellers who find their buyers have breached the contract by refusing to close would be better off quitting any claim to the deposit money and finding another buyer. When angry sellers file a lawsuit to collect the deposit money, the buyers may have no alternative but to countersue. The ensuing legal action creates what is known as a "cloud" on the property's title, making it impossible for a title company to issue a policy and another buyer to close on the property until the matter is resolved. Despite what your lawyer promises, know that the wheels of justice turn very, very slowly.

Even if a buyer deliberately fails to close, the courts usually require sellers to "mitigate damages" before seeking relief in the courts. That is, the court expects sellers to relist their home and find another buyer and do all they can to avoid or lessen their financial harm.

Sellers can have an easier time gaining possession of the deposit money if they include a "liquidated damages" provision in their contract of sale. The term "liquidated damages" means the buyer and seller have agreed that the deposit money will be the amount of compensation should the contract be breached. This eliminates the need for a trial to establish damages.

Your agent ought to confirm each step of the transaction with you as it progresses toward the closing and know the warning signs of problem buyers:

✓ A negative first impression

✓ Bellicose when negotiating the sales contract

✓ Late scheduling inspections or applying for the loan

✓ Numerous visits to the home *after* the contract is signed

✓ Unreasonable about home-inspection repairs

✓ Their agent stops communicating with your agent

✓ Requests multiple extensions of the closing date

✓ They have a problem scheduling the closing no one can explain.

Serving Time Is of the Essence

The closing date agreed to on your contract may be rescheduled during the course of the transaction without much worry. However, a repeated postponement usually means the buyer has a serious problem. Be wary of buyers or their agent making endless promises about resolving a problem but never offering a solution. They may lead you on for weeks while your home is off the market and your plans are put on hold.

The failure of one party to perform by a specific date specified in a contract of sale is not considered a breach unless the contract contains the following: "Time is of the essence, and all dates set forth in this contract are exact." This dictates that all the dates and time limits governing the actions of both buyer and seller *must occur exactly when specified* or the other party will have grounds to seek damages.

Be warned, serving "time is of the essence" is a dangerous legal procedure that should only be used as a last resort and with the guidance of an attorney. "Time is of the essence" holds both buyer and seller to the same standard. Secondly, it changes the tone of the transaction where the serving party adopts a bellicose position, forcing the other to react accordingly.

Last-Minute Postponement of Closing

Avoid use and occupancy agreements and allowing the buyers and/or their belongings to move into your home before title closes and you get paid. Should you permit the buyers use of your home prior to closing because of some snafu, it may be extremely difficult to evict them if the closing is eventually cancelled.

(COMPLAINT PHASE)

40
CHAPTER

How to Fire Your Listing Agent

As explained in Chapter 13, most listing contracts only require the agent to upload your home to MLS, so when you attempt to fire the agent for an unfulfilled promise, you have no evidence the agent made the promise.

I know an angry seller trapped in an unbreakable listing contract who exacted revenge by building a website with a name like www.mybrokersucks.com. Despite the website, the broker refused to terminate the listing contract. To avoid such battles, never sign a listing contract that lasts more than ninety days or one that does not have a provision for early termination. See Chapter 13, "The Tricks and Traps of the Listing Contract".

If you foolishly signed an unbreakable listing contract, the best time to dismiss the agent is immediately following a significant snafu:

✓ A failure to present an offer.

✓ Lack of promised advertising or service.

✓ An unethical or illegal act.

✓ A substantial omission from the MLS data sheet, i.e., no photos.

✓ A failure to install lockbox or showing instructions for buyer agents.

When attempting to cancel a listing contract, the squeaky wheel gets the grease. But before writing a poison-pen letter, contact your agent and ask to be released. No honest agent wants an unhappy client.

The agent may claim the release must be approved by the office manager or the broker-owner of the firm. When this happens, the agent and her firm may work together and stall for time in hopes a buyer will appear before the listing expires or that you will just give up. Be persistent.

If you want to be released because you have your own buyer and did not make a provision in the listing contract for selling to your own buyer, do not bother asking. When an agent suspects a seller wants to sell to his own buyer to avoid paying a commission, the agent will dig in his heels and wait until the listing expires—no matter how long it takes.

Be Certain You Are Released from the Listing Contract

Shady Agents who agree to "withdraw" your listing from MLS database may deceive you into thinking you have been released from the listing contract but in reality you are still obligated to pay a commission should the house sell. Merely withdrawing or removing your home from MLS and Realtor.com does release you from the original listing contract and paying a commission.

Worse, when your listing agent removes or "withdraws" your home from MLS and you then relist with another agency without being released in writing from the original listing contract, you will be obligated to pay two commissions: one to your new broker and another to your original broker who "withdrew" the listing from MLS.

Carefully read paperwork an agent claims you must to sign to terminate the listing. Be certain the documents do not include the word "conditional." The document must "release" you from the listing contract. Shady Agents will try to charge a "termination fee"—do not pay it.

Sample Listing Agreement Termination Letter with Release

Dear Shady Agent Realty:

This letter will serve to confim you agree to terminate our listing contract. Effective immediately you agree to withdraw my property from the MLS database and release me from the listing contract and any and all obligations to pay you or your firm a commission or any termination fee.

Very truly yours,

_____

Seller

_____

Listing Agency

41
CHAPTER

Filing a Complaint with the Board of Realtors

Consumers looking for relief or justice should know their local Board of Realtors is a private corporation affiliated with the trade group known as the National Association of Realtors (NAR). Essentially, a local Board of Realtors is a fundraising arm of the NAR and a social club for real estate agents. Any organization using the term "Realtor" is *not* a government agency and does not have the power to enforce licensing laws or revoke the license of a broker or agent.

Do not confuse the NAR affiliated "Board of Realtors" with the governmental regulatory "Boards" found in New York State, Virginia, Wisconsin, Massachusetts, Canada, and Australia.

Agents and brokers that operate and oversee the Realtor board are unpaid volunteers. Filing a complaint against a member of the Board of Realtors may be a waste of time because Realtors are reluctant to find fault with their own dues-paying members. They avoid responding to complaints in writing, preferring to talk on the phone. Most times they ignore you in hopes you go away or that the offending agent resolves the problem.

However, when a local board office acknowledges your complaint, their grievance committee will determine if the offending Realtor member violated the Realtor code of ethics. If the committee believes a violation occurred, a hearing could be held with you and the Realtor to resolve or mediate the dispute.

If the hearing finds the Realtor violated the code of ethics, the board will likely mail a letter to the offending agent stating the agent violated the code and hope the embarrassment may be enough for the agent to correct the wrong.

Realtors claim their members may be "fined, reprimanded, or their membership suspended or terminated for serious or repeated violations" of their code of ethics. However, the local board has no authority to force Realtor members to pay damages and cannot suspend or revoke an agent's license.

In the event the board believes the member's misdeed violates the law, the board will hopefully report its findings to the state department of real estate. A Realtor's membership in the club would probably be revoked only if the state authority revoked the agent's license. Consumers should file their complaint with the government agency that issues real estate licenses—more on this in the next chapter.

42
CHAPTER

Filing a Complaint with the Licensing Agency

Neither the trade group known as the National Association of Realtors (NAR) nor its local affiliated boards of Realtors has any legal authority over licensed brokers or agents. Only the state real estate commission or department of real estate that issues licenses can suspend or revoke them. Be warned that you cannot expect perfection or achieve closure from licensing agencies because those who operate them have little real estate sales experience and are hired or appointed by a political body.

When you file a complaint, the agency may investigate the licensee, but the agency is not a court of law and does not award damages. However, aggrieved consumers may receive financial restitution if a licensee has stolen deposit or escrow money. That money may be reimbursed by a special fund administered by the licensing agency.

Licensing authorities will not discipline or revoke an agent's license because he/she was rude or did a lousy job selling your home. Not returning phone calls and acting like a jackass may be bad business, but it is not illegal.

Reasons Agents May Face Disciplinary Action or Lose Their License

✓ Commingling of funds. A licensee cannot commingle your money with his or his firm's checking accounts at any time. It must be kept in a separate escrow account that has been registered with the licensing agency.

✓ Failing to collect the deposit money or account for same.

✓ Making false promises or false representations. For example, an agent claims the buyers do not require a mortgage loan as they are paying cash, only to find they cannot close because they have no cash.

✓ Failing to present all offers, including subsequent offers. Many jurisdictions extend this to include verbal offers.

✓ Receiving a commission or fee from more than one party to a transaction without the prior consent of all parties.

✓ Collecting a commission from an associated party to the transaction without the client's knowledge. For example, an agent recommends you use her brother's title company, who then quietly pays the agent a fee.

✓ Flagrantly misrepresenting facts. For example, the MLS data sheet claims the property is located in a specific sought-after school district when in fact it is not.

✓ Conduct showing incompetence, dishonesty, or bad faith. This is a common charged levied by against agents who do not protect their clients' best interests.

✓ Failing to cooperate with a licensing authority subpoena.

✓ Failing to deliver a copy of a listing or sales contract to a party of the document. Consumers must receive a copy of every document they sign.

✓ Failing to provide a termination date on the listing contract.

✓ Using a drawing or offering prizes as a promotion, e.g., "Come to our open house and win a HDTV".

✓ Not disclosing a prior or pending criminal conviction when applying for a license.

✓ Using a trade name when the agent is not a member, e.g., an agent cannot claim to be a member of a professional organization unless he/she is a member of that organization.

✓ Paying a kickback or referral fee to anyone without a license, e.g., an agent gives money or finder's fee to an unlicensed friend who recommended the agent.

✓ Collecting a commission or fee from anyone except the employing broker of record or owner of the firm, e.g., the agent collects a fee or commission without his/her broker's knowledge.

✓ Failing to keep a client informed, e.g., an agent fails to notify the seller that the buyer cannot obtain the loan to complete the purchase.

✓ Discriminating against anyone based on race, creed, color, national origin, sex, marital status, affection or sexual orientation, familial status, physical or mental disability, ancestry, nationality, domestic partners, those with HIV or AIDS, or those receiving financial aid from the federal agency known as HUD.

How to File Your Complaint

Some states or provinces have a complaint form on their website. Some jurisdictions like Florida keep all complaints confidential. Others post a list of disciplined licensees with no explanation of the crime. The website addresses and phone numbers of the licensing authorities in the United States are listed at the end of this chapter.

Resist calling the licensing authority and relating a long and tedious story. Instead, complete a complaint form or type a letter. Be chronological and to the point. Include copies of the listing agreement, contract of sale, letters, closing statement, and the MLS data sheet. Include all your contact numbers, as investigators may not pursue the complaint unless they can get your help in getting all the facts.

The investigator's job is to gather facts and then deliver those facts to his or her superior, who may or may not take action. The authority will only take action if the agent or broker's action is a violation of the law. They will do nothing about an agent's rude behavior or the fact that the agent failed to sell your home. They will not enforce any terms of a contract. They will first determine if the complaint is a civil matter to be adjudicated in a civil court before they consider bringing any action against the licensee.

If the agent has financially damaged you, seek the aid of an attorney. The licensing authority cannot award you monetary damages unless the agent misappropriated (stole) your deposit or escrow money. If that happens, the government licensing agency usually has a fund specifically designed to replenish lost deposit money.

Sample Complaint Letter to the Government Licensing Agency

To the State Real Estate Commission or Department of Real Estate:

Dear Investigations,

I wish to file a complaint against real estate agent Jane Doe who prepared a fraudulent commission statement and collected $3,250.00 more than what she was entitled to. Jane Doe also prepared the contract of sale that correctly stated the commission as $4,750.00.

I did not notice the overpayment until after the closing. When I called agent Jane Doe to ask for a refund, she said could not pay me because the house had already closed.

Sincerely,

Seller
123 Mocking Bird Lane
Your Town
999-1212 cell

Actual Disciplinary Actions

Arizona—Marijohn Kirkland - Salesperson's License SA562176000 - The respondent represented an individual on a sale of property. Ms. Kirkland removed approximately $1,000 worth of furniture and personal possessions from the seller's residence without permission. The licensee was directed to return all items by her designated broker and failed to do so.

Arkansas—In Formal Hearing #2055 the Commissioners voted that "…Respondent Mary L. Gruber be issued a Letter of Reprimand to be placed in her license file, and that she is required to take the 30-hour broker course…Gruber is to pay a fine of $500.00 within thirty (30) days of receipt of notice of this hearing decision." The Commission found Gruber guilty of violating Commission Regulation 8.5 (a). Gruber did not protect and promote the interests of her client (Seller) as follows: 1. She did not include any provision in either of the counteroffers to Buyers A or Buyers B to protect Complainant (Seller) from having both buyers accept the respective counteroffers with the result that Complainant would have two real estate contracts to sell her property to the two different buyers. 2. She faxed the Complainant's counteroffer for Buyer B to the selling agent Principal Broker when she knew that Buyers A had verbally accepted their counteroffer and without notifying Complainant of that verbal acceptance or addressing with the Complainant whether to withdraw or modify her counteroffer to Buyer B. 3. She failed to take reasonable action to withdraw Complainant's counteroffer to Buyer B by delivering notice of Buyer B's withdrawal to Principal Broker prior to Buyer B's acceptance of that counteroffer being communicated to Respondent Gruber.

Colorado—Rex W. Brandt licensee (Complaint # 2007101934) engaged in a transaction that included undisclosed buyer rebates: a $250,000 payment allegedly for landscape and a pool Brandt receive as a buyer, failed to disclose funds to purchaser without adequate disclosure to lender, failed to disclose brokerage relationships in writing, failed to maintain files as required, and failed to ensure settlement statements. Mr. Brandt's real estate license shall be revoked; and he shall pay a fine of $46,000.

Iowa—Randy S. Wilson. The Applicant does not contest that he failed to accurately disclose his criminal history as requested by question 10a on the license application form. The Applicant voluntarily agrees that as a condition for receiving a new Iowa real estate salesperson license, the Applicant shall pay to the Commission a civil monetary penalty in the amount of five hundred dollars ($500.00) within 30 days of the Commission's approval of this Agreement.

Illinois—Kevin Maloney, license (476-381650) placed on probation for two years and fined $2,500 for acting outside the scope of his salesperson license, specifically owning and operating two web sites, engaged in leasing condominium apartment units, held security deposits without an escrow account and co-mingled funds with his personal accounts.

New Jersey—Nirva Tullis, salesperson, Somerset County—On May 13, 2008, the Commission approved a consent agreement whereby Nirva Tullis agreed to a one-year revocation of her salesperson's license and a $1,000 fine. Ms. Tullis admitted to violating N.J.S.A. 45:15-17(a), N.J.S.A. 45:15-17(e), and N.J.S.A. 45:15-17(l). She fraudulently signed listing agreements on behalf of four sellers who were not aware that their homes were being listed for sale. The listings were promptly withdrawn when her broker became aware of her activities. George Kacprzykowski, formerly licensed New Jersey real estate salesperson, Burlington County—By Final Order dated October 9, 2012, the Commission determined Kacprzykowski's conviction of theft by deception arising out of his real estate brokerage business demonstrated unworthiness, bad faith and dishonesty in violation of N.J.S.A. 45:15-17(e) and such conduct established that Kacprzykowski did not possess good character, honesty, integrity and trustworthiness required under N.J.S.A. 45:15-9. The Commission also found that Kacpryzykowski's eligibility for a real estate license was subject to revocation pursuant to N.J.S.A. 45:15-19.1 because he had been convicted of a theft offense which was related to his activities as a real estate salesperson. His failure to notify the Commission within 30 days of the filing of those criminal charges against him was a violation of N.J.S.A. 45:15-17(s). Kacprzykowski's failure to account for or pay over escrow money in a real estate transaction and his commingling of those funds with his own were violations of N.J.S.A. 45:15-17 (d), (t) and (o). Kacprzykowski's conduct demonstrated he engaged in dishonest dealing in violation of N.J.S.A. 45:15-17(l). The Commission permanently revoked Kacprzykowski's real estate salesperson's license and imposed a fine of $25,000.

New Mexico—The New Mexico Real Estate Commission revoked the real estate broker's licenses of John and Barbara Walterick, the former owner/operators of Mountain Valley Realtors in Edgewood. The commission also imposed more than $4,000 in fines and administrative hearing costs on the Waltericks and ordered that Barbara Walterick must satisfy the terms of previous disciplinary orders before she can apply again for a real estate broker's license. The commission found that Barbara Walterick continued to practice real estate for more than two years after her broker's license was suspended by the commission. After her license was suspended and subsequently expired, her husband, John Walterick, became the qualifying broker for Mountain Valley Realtors and permitted his wife to continue to work for Mountain Valley as a real estate broker, according to the commission's findings. In 2006, the commission served three separate disciplinary action notices on the couple over real estate transactions in which the Waltericks and Mountain Valley Realtors were involved after Mrs. Walterick's license expired. In October 2003, Barbara Walterick was ordered to serve two consecutive six-month suspensions, pay administrative penalties totaling $1,000, and make restitution of $1,300 to clients for violations of the commission's property-management rules. She never paid those fines or the restitution ordered, according to Real Estate Commission Executive Director Wayne Ciddio. In 2002, she received a letter of reprimand from the commission for violations of property-management rules. It is illegal to engage in real estate activities in New Mexico without a license and illegal for a qualifying broker to allow unlicensed persons to practice under the qualifying broker's license, Ciddio noted. It is also illegal for a brokerage to pay unlicensed persons commissions on real estate transactions.

Pennsylvania—Rene J. Fougeray Jr., license no. RB047093L, of Lehighton, Carbon County, was reprimanded and assessed a $1,000 civil penalty based on findings that Fougeray demonstrated bad faith, dishonestly, untrustworthiness, or incompetency in a real estate transaction for failing to include required provisions in and placing buyers' initials on the Agreement of Sale without their authorization.

Texas—James Robert Willoughby (Austin), License #348568, acting negligently or incompetently in a transaction by using a combination lockbox on a property that allowed a buyer and perhaps others unlimited access to the property without any licensee's knowledge of the access, in violation of §1101.652(b)(1) of the Texas Occupations Code; engaging in conduct that constitutes dishonest dealings, bad faith, or untrustworthiness in a transaction when, while acting as a listing agent, salesperson misled sellers that a buyer representative was involved in the transaction when in fact salesperson was the only salesperson involved, was dealing directly with buyers, received both sides of the commission, and also received a $2,000.00 bonus intended for the selling agent, in violation of §1101.652(b)(2) of the Texas Occupations Code; failing to obtain from buyers their written consent to an intermediary relationship, in violation of §1101.559 of the Texas Occupations Code; failing to be faithful and observant to trust placed in the agent and to be scrupulous and meticulous in performing the agent's functions in a real estate transaction by submitting inaccurate and misleading contract documents for review and signature by the principals, in violation of 22 TAC §531.1(2); advertising brokerage activity by using a name other than the name in which the salesperson was licensed, in violation of 22 TAC §535.154(c); placing brokerage advertisements that imply that the salesperson is the person responsible for the operation of a real estate brokerage, in violation of 22 TAC §535.154(e); placing brokerage advertisements on the Internet that do not include on each page information required by the Rules of the Commission, in violation of 22 TAC §535.154(i). Agreed six-month suspension of salesperson license fully probated for two years, effective July 28, 2008; agreed administrative penalty of $7,000, entered July 28, 2008.

Washington, DC—Marisa L. Bronfman. By consent order, respondent agreed to pay a fine in the amount of $2,500 with the stipulation of release from any charges without admission of liability. The following charges were served on the respondent: 1) failure to deposit monies within seven days in an account in an insured financial institution in the District of Columbia, in violation of DC official code section-1704 (a)(10) (2001); 2) failure to account for or remit any money, valuable document, or other property coming in to her possession, which belonged to others in a reasonable time in violation of DC official code section 47-2853.197(10)(2001); and 3) failure to exercise ordinary care as a real estate broker on behalf of buyers, in violation of DC official code section 47-2853.192(d)(4)(2001).

<u>Where to File Your Complaint</u>

Follows is a list of government real estate authorities in the United States where you can direct a complaint against a licensed agent or broker.

Alabama Real Estate Commission
1201 Carmichael Way
Montgomery, AL 36106
(334) 242-5544
www.arec.state.al.us

Alaska Real Estate Commission
Robert B. Atwood Building
550 W. 7th Avenue, Suite 1950
Anchorage, AK 99501
(907) 269-8160
www.dced.state.ak.us/occ/prec19.htm

Arizona Department of Real Estate
2910 N. 44th Street
Phoenix, AZ 85018
(602) 771-7750
www.re.state.az.us

Arkansas Real Estate Commission
612 South Summit Street
Little Rock, AR 72201-4740
(501) 683-8010
www.state.ar.us/arec/arecweb.html

California Department of Real Estate
2201 Broadway
Sacramento, CA 95818-2500
(877) 373-4542
www.dre.ca.gov/

Colorado Division of Real Estate
1560 Broadway, Suite 925
Denver, CO 80202
(303) 894-2166
www.dora.state.co.us/real-estate

Connecticut Department of Consumer Protection
Real Estate Trade Practices Division
165 Capitol Avenue—Room 110
Hartford, CT 06106
(860) 713-6300
www.state.ct.us/dcp

Delaware Division of Professional Regulation
Investigative Supervisor
861 Silver Lake Blvd., Suite 203
Dover, DE 19904-2467
(302) 744-4509
www.dpr.delaware.gov/boards/realestate/

District of Columbia Board of Real Estate
941 North Capitol Street NE, 7th Floor
Washington, DC 20002
(202) 442-4340
No website

Florida Division of Real Estate
Attention: Consumer Complaints Section
400 West Robinson Street, N801
Orlando, FL 32801
(850) 487-1395
www.myflorida.com/dbpr/re

Georgia Real Estate Commission
229 Peachtree Street NE
International Tower, Suite 1000
Atlanta, GA 30303-1605
(404) 656-3916
www.grec.state.ga.us/
Hawaii Real Estate Branch
Supervising Investigator
Consumer Resource Center
Regulated Industries Complaints Office

Department of Commerce & Consumer Affairs
235 S. Beretania Street, 9th Floor
Honolulu, HI 96813
(808) 587-3222 or (808) 586-2653
www.hawaii.gov/hirec/

Idaho Real Estate Commission
633 North 4th Street
PO Box 83720
Boise, ID 83720-0077
(208) 334-3285
http://www.idahorealestatecommission.com

Illinois Division of Professional Regulation
James R. Thompson Center
100 W. Randolph Street Suite 9-300
Chicago, IL 60601
(312) 814-4500
www.idfpr.com/dpr/RE/REALEST.asp

Indiana Professional Licensing Agency
Attn: Indiana Real Estate Commission
402 West Washington Street, Room W072
Indianapolis, IN 46204
(317) 234-3009
http://www.in.gov/pla/real.htm

Iowa Real Estate Commission
1920 SE Hulsizer Road
Ankeny, IA 50021-3941
(515) 281-7382
www.state.ia.us/government/com/prof/sales

Kansas Real Estate Commission
Three Townsite Plaza, Suite 200
120 SE 6th Ave
Topeka, KS 66603-3511
(785) 296-3411
www.kansas.gov/krec/

Kentucky Real Estate Commission
10200 Linn Station Road, Suite 201
Louisville, KY 40223

(888) 373-3300
www.krec.ky.gov

Louisiana Real Estate Commission
9071 Interline Avenue
PO Box 14785
Baton Rouge, LA 70898-4785
(800) 821-4529
www.lrec.state.la.us/

Maine Office of Licensing and Registration
Department of Professional & Financial Regulation
Office of Licensing & Registration
35 State House Station
Augusta, ME 04333-0035
(207) 624-8524
www.maine.gov/pfr/professionallicensing

Maryland Division of Occupational and Professional Licensing
500 North Calvert Street
Baltimore, MD 21202-3651
(410) 230-6230
www.dllr.state.md.us/license/occprof/recomm.html

Massachusetts Division of Professional Licensure
239 Causeway Street, Suite 500
Boston, MA 02114
(617) 727-7406
www.mass.gov/dpl

Michigan Department of Labor & Economic Growth
Bureau of Commercial Services - Enforcement Division
P.O. Box 30018
Lansing, MI 48909
(517) 241-9202
www.michigan.gov/

Minnesota Department of Commerce
Market Assurance Division
85 7th Place East, Suite 600
St. Paul, MN 55101
(651) 296-2488
www.state.mn.us/

Mississippi Real Estate Commission
P.O. Box 12685
Jackson, MS 39236
(601) 932-6770
www.mrec.state.ms.us
Missouri Real Estate Commission
3605 Missouri Boulevard
PO Box 1339
Jefferson City, MO 65102-1339
(573) 751-2628
http://pr.mo.gov/realestate.asp

Montana Board of Realty Regulation
Business Standards Division
301 S. Park, 4th Floor
PO Box 200513
Helena, MT 59602
(406) 841-2336
www.mt.gov/dli/rre/

Nevada Real Estate Division
2501 East Sahara Avenue, Suite 102
Las Vegas, NV 89104-4137
(702) 486-4033
www.red.state.nv.us/realestate/re_commission.htm

Nebraska Real Estate Commission
1200 N Street, Suite 402
P.O. Box 94667
Lincoln, NE 68509-4667
(402) 471-2004
www.nol.org/home/NREC/index.htm

New Hampshire Real Estate Commission
State House Annex, Room 434
25 Capitol Street
Concord, NH 03301
(603) 271-2703
www.nh.gov/nhrec/

New Jersey Real Estate Commission
CN-328
Trenton, NJ 08625

(609) 292-7272
www.state.nj.us/dobi/division_rec/

New Mexico Real Estate Commission
5200 Oakland Ave. NE, Suite #B
Albuquerque, NM 87113
(800) 801-7505
www.rld.state.nm.us/RealEstateCommission

New York Department of State
Division of Licensing Services
P.O. Box 22001
Albany, NY 12201-2001
(518) 474-4429
http://www.dos.state.ny.us/cnsl/complain.html

North Carolina Real Estate Commission
P.O. Box 17100
Raleigh, NC 27619-7100
(919) 875-3700
www.ncrec.state.nc.us

North Dakota Real Estate Commission
200 East Main Avenue, Suite 204
PO Box 727
Bismarck, ND 58501
(701) 328-9749
www.realestatend.org

Ohio Department of Commerce
Division of Real Estate & Professional Licensing
77 South High Street, 20th Floor
Columbus, OH 43215-6133
(614) 466-4100
www.com.ohio.gov/real/

Oklahoma Real Estate Commission
Investigations Department
2401 NW 23rd Street, Suite 18
Oklahoma City, OK 73107
(405) 521-3387
www.orec.state.ok.us

Oregon Real Estate Board
1177 Center St. NE
Salem, OR 97301-2505
(503) 378-4170
www.oregon.gov/REA/

Pennsylvania Real Estate Commission
P.O. Box 2649
Harrisburg, PA 17105-2649
(717) 783-3658
(717) 783-4849: Complaint Hotline
www.dos.state.pa.us/bpoa

Texas Real Estate Commission
P. O. Box 12188
Austin, TX 78711-2188
512-936-3000
www.trec.state.tx.us

Vermont Real Estate Commission
Vermont Secretary of State
Office of Professional Regulation
National Life Bldg., FL2
Montpelier, VT 05620-3402
(802) 828-2808
www.vtprofessionals.org/opr1/real_estate/

West Virginia Real Estate Commission
300 Capitol Street, Suite 400
Charleston, WV 25301
(304) 558-3555
www.wvrec.org

Wyoming Real Estate Commission
2020 Carey Avenue, Suite 702
Cheyenne, WY 82002-0180
(307) 777-7141
http://realestate.state.wy.us/

About the Author

Slick Shyster owned and operated a real estate brokerage for over 30 years until being sued for fraud. Slick was also an adjunct professor of Real Estate Practices and a property manager for the US Department of Veterans Affairs.

Comments and questions welcomed: slick@shadyagents.com.

This book is available at Amazon.com.

www.ingramcontent.com/pod-product-compliance
Lightning Source LLC
Chambersburg PA
CBHW081448170526
45166CB00008B/2360